THE BEST
IS YET TO BE

Other Books by Martin Down

Speak To These Bones
Streams Of Living Water
Building A New Church Alongside The Old
Deluded By Darwinism?
The New Jerusalem
Low Cost - High Price (with Theresa Cumbers)
Love Each Other

THE BEST
IS YET TO BE

Being happy in retirement and old age

By

MARTIN DOWN

emblembooks

www.emblembooks.co.uk

ISBN 978-0-9559594-7-9

Cover design by Adam Jackson.

Published by Emblem Books, Ashill, UK
www.emblembooks.co.uk

Contents

Chapter One

INTRODUCTION

Retirement is one of the major transitions in modern life: puberty, starting work, marriage, children – retirement. But retirement is probably the one for which we are least prepared.

We almost certainly spent years looking forward to the next of these earlier transitions and making plans for it, at least in our imagination. But from the point of view of the working man or the working woman, retirement is simply the end of the road.

We may have a variety of feelings about the end of this road, but we are probably too busy to give much thought to where the road might lead after that. The retirement age is like the brow of a hill: until we reach it, it is difficult to see what lies over the other side.

The retirement age is a very arbitrary milestone. The government can alter at will the point at which it awards us an Old Age Pension.

The best is yet to be

There is nothing particularly significant about sixty or sixty-five or any other anniversary; in some positions an occupational pension is paid at fifty-five or even earlier. But at whatever age we retire we do not suddenly change into another person on a particular birthday.

For most of us retirement means that life undergoes a radical change, but the change is in our outward circumstances, not in who we are. Our finances change; our housing may change; we will spend more time with our husbands or wives, if we have them; we will have more time at our own disposal. But the biggest challenge is to the way in which we see ourselves. Lee Iacocca, one-time CEO of Chrysler, wrote about retirement: 'Everybody says you've got to get ready financially. No, no, you've got to get ready psychologically.'

I am aware that I am writing this book from a male point of view. As a man, I could hardly do otherwise. But I am aware also that there are different transitions in the life of a woman, and that retirement is not perhaps as significant a milestone in the life of a woman as it is in that of a man.

Putting it the other way round, there is no real equivalent for men of the female menopause. There may be a male mid-life crisis, in which a man realises that 'this is probably it' in terms of his career, and that the remaining years of his working life are probably only going to mean more of the same. But for a woman, the mid-life transition of the menopause is a much greater physical and psychological turning point.

At the risk of being dismissed as hopelessly sexist and chauvinistic, I would guess that a man finds a larger part of his identity in his work than a woman does and that, conversely, a woman finds a larger part of her identity in her children and home than a man.

So, dear woman, if you pick up this book about retirement and find that it does not speak to your condition, please forgive me and try to find something else that does. Have you discovered Jane Shilling's *The Stranger in the Mirror,* a touchingly honest examination of the onset of middle age in a woman, though without resolution?

Whether you are a man or a woman, however, contemplating either the crisis of the menopause or the crisis of retirement, the most important thing, psychologically, is not to think that it is all over. There is still plenty to do and plenty to achieve after the age of fifty or sixty or sixty-five, or whatever, if we want to do it.

Margaret Thatcher did not become Prime Minister until she was fifty-four and continued until she was sixty-six. Winston Churchill did not become the great war-time Prime Minister of Britain that he was until he was sixty-five. Nelson Mandela did not become the first black president of the Republic of South Africa until he was seventy-five.

I myself was on my way to speak at a conference in Finland at the age of seventy. I was killing time between flights at Helsinki airport, on a grey, wet afternoon. I was thinking to myself, 'I am getting too old for this,' when a thought dropped into my head that I believe came from God: 'John Wesley was still in the saddle at eighty-nine. What's the matter with you?'

That moment my attitude to retirement changed miraculously. I stopped thinking that I was basically finished. You may be retired but you are not finished.

Introduction

And yet, retirement is not just more of the same. It is new beginning. It is different; and it is not easy.

Chapter Two

THE BIG ISSUE

The golden years, a time of opportunity, a whole new life awaiting you: these are some of the ways in which retirement is sold to you in the books that you find in the bookshop or the public library.

The ones that I have consulted are mines of information about everything, from how to manage your investments, to how to contact *The Basketmakers Association*. I assume that the latter was included in case the reader wanted to take up basket making, rather than because they expected to end up in a basket.

But that raises a question about these popular books: positive they may be about old age, but they almost entirely ignore the challenges that retirement brings. They are, more often than not, hopelessly unrealistic about old age, pretending that this stage of our lives is just another chance to get and spend money, to improve our homes and gardens, to indulge in new hobbies and more and more travel.

They may include tips for keeping fit and eating healthy meals, and advice about regular trips to the dentist, the optician and the chiropodist - a nod in the direction of the fact that we may not be as fit as we used to be. But real discussion of increasing infirmity and ill-health takes place only in terms of caring for aged parents, ignoring the fact that at this time of our lives it is more likely that we are the aged parents who will need to be cared for.

In short, most books about retirement encourage us to maintain the illusion that our lives are going to go on and on forever in much the same way as they have done for the last forty or fifty years, except that we no longer have to go to work. The only significant changes that we need to make are financial ones, and otherwise it will be sunshine and roses all the way.

In a poem called *Rabbi ben Ezra,* Robert Browning wrote these wonderful lines, a positive outlook on old age if ever there was one, yet an outlook that transcends the clichés of the 21st century:

The best is yet to be

Grow old along with me!
The best is yet to be,
The last of life for which the first was made:
Our times are in his hand
Who saith, 'A whole I planned,
Youth shows but half: trust God;
see all, nor be afraid!'

I do trust God; I am not afraid of growing old; but neither am I starry-eyed about it. We need to 'see all' about retirement, not just one half of it.

I do not believe that we can enjoy 'the last of life' until we have faced up to its challenges, which are as great as any that we faced in our youth or at any other stage of our long lives so far. In this book, we shall indeed study the question of how to make the most of the opportunities that retirement brings, and how to make these years as golden as possible.

But we shall also look at some of the harder issues of retirement and old age: what am I worth without my work, how do I cope with feelings of disappointment, what do I do with my memories of sin and failure, how can I enjoy seeing young people falling in love, having babies and doing all the things I used to do, or did not do, but am now too old to do? And how do I face up to the biggest issue of all, my own mortality.

We cannot really deal with any of the issues facing us in retirement until we have dealt with this last one, because it will affect the reasons and the way in which we do everything else. Are our activities in retirement merely distractions to stop us considering the reality of death? Is increased leisure-time in retirement only going to open the door to feelings of despair? How can we grow old gracefully and happily with death hanging over us?

That is the Big Issue.

We live in a culture which discourages us from thinking or talking about death. Many people resolutely refuse to face up to it, even during their terminal illnesses. They and their friends and relations are determined to keep up the pretence that 'Granny is going to get better and will soon be up and about.'

Granny knows in her heart that she won't, but if she wants to talk about death, the chances are that she will be told not to be morbid. Now, there is such a thing as morbidness but it is not a fault to which most people in 21st century Western culture are prone. On the contrary, our fault is that we do not think or talk enough about death, and we do not think about it early enough for it make a difference to our values and the way we live our lives.

But if we have never thought about death before, we need to start thinking about it in retirement, because the next stop is the crematorium or the graveyard. The truth for us is that one day in the not too distant future the world is going to stop, and we need to be ready to get off.

So in thinking about retirement we must start with the Big Issue: we are mortal. One day in old age, if we have not done it before, we are going to die. Before that day, mortality also means that as we grow older our bodies are going to decay; they will slow down; bits of them will drop off, wear out, or fail.

If we cannot handle these truths about the human condition, then all our activities and occupations will be mere escapism and self-deception.

Of course, none of us can finally escape these truths. During the silent hours of the night, if not at other times during the day, thoughts of infirmity and death will come back to haunt us however hard we try to suppress them, and have probably been doing so since our youth. What we need is help in facing up to them and living with them, with faith and without fear.

This is what the average secular book about retirement does not even begin to offer, and yet until we have tackled the Big Issue we are not in a fit state to deal with any of the lesser ones.

Every stage of life brings its own challenges, and this, above all, is the challenge of old age. Of course, it would be a good thing if we had faced up to our mortality much earlier in life than this; if we have not done so we may find that much of our lives has been wasted, because we have been living according to false values or living for merely passing pleasures.

But retirement and old age bring us face to face with the issue of our own mortality in a new and immediate way. It is now undeniable that we are on the last lap of the race, or at least the last lap but one.

Old age may be divided into two parts: the years of active and healthy old age, and the years of declining health and infirmity. There is not usually a sudden break between these two phases; old age is a continuum of the two in different proportions.

There was a period in history in which people deliberately lived with a *memento mori*, a reminder of death, perhaps a skull on the table or beside the bed. That seems today to be unbearably ghoulish, and yes, morbid, but to banish the very thought of death from our lives and particularly from our lives in retirement, as many books about retirement encourage us to do, is simply to bury our heads in the sand, and to condemn ourselves to a life of unreality.

The only acknowledgement of our own impending death that is made in most books about retirement is advice about making a will for the benefit of those we leave behind, and making known our wishes about the funeral. These are indeed important preparations to make, but they do not touch the core of our need to face our own demise.

The secret that we need to discover is how to live our last years with the knowledge of our finitude and mortality and yet not to live them in gloom and misery but to live them happily and fully.

The question of whether we can do this or not depends on what we believe about death. Is it the end? Or is there something to come afterwards? Do we have to resign ourselves to declining powers and pleasures or, as Browning says, is the best yet to be?

There is, out there, a supermarket of ideas, beliefs and superstitions about what happens when you die. Some people, influenced by Hinduism, Buddhism, and other Eastern religions, believe in reincarnation: that death is simply the end of one turn on the merry-go-round of life, before we pay our penny or our pound and have another go, in another time and another place, in another body and under another name.

Since for everyone life is a mixture of pleasure and pain, of fulfilment and disappointment, of prosperity and hardship, that is hardly an encouraging or reassuring prospect, especially since for a great many people in the world there seems to be more of the latter than the former. What people in the West do not realise is that in the East reincarnation is regarded as a curse not a blessing: the aim of Eastern religion is to escape the cycle of reincarnation, not to perpetuate it.

Moslems, on the other hand, believe that men, at least, if they have lived good lives or died as martyrs, may go to a Paradise where they are waited upon by 'immortal youths and dark-eyed houris'[1]; whether anyone has lived a good enough life or whether this is Paradise for the immortal youths and dark-eyed houris is not so clear.

Other people, influenced by spiritualism, believe that the dead live on in some disembodied form, hanging around in the wings, waiting to deliver trivial messages to the living. Judging by the notes and epitaphs left behind on the bunches of flowers, and inscribed on gravestones in memory of the dear departed, the most popular belief in Britain today is that when we die we become stars in the sky or angels in heaven.

Some people are explicit in their rejection of any continuation of life after death at all. 'When you're dead you're dead,' they say. But that is as much a matter of faith as any other belief.

---

[1] *The Koran*, Sura 56:15-36.

Christians believe in the resurrection of the dead and the life of the world to come.

It is no easy matter to sort through this jumble of contradictory beliefs and dogmas, and most people, understandably, shelve the question as too difficult, and resolve to wait and see. But agnosticism is no more comforting or hopeful in our declining years than outright atheism. The end result is the same: 'eat, drink and be merry, for tomorrow we die.'

The trouble is that eating and drinking then become just that very escapism upon which we remarked earlier: it is impossible to be truly merry with the prospect of death hanging over us. And there is yet another possibility in the spectrum of beliefs about life after death, a possibility that the modern world has done its best to banish from its thoughts altogether: the suffering of everlasting pangs of remorse and despair, the fires of hell.

So perhaps the first challenge of retirement is to think carefully and seriously about the future and what lies ahead of us in terms of life and death. There may be those who want to examine all the options, but in the nature of the case, the difficulty of making up our minds between them is likely to fill the casual enquirer with despair.

Is there any hard evidence, as opposed to wishful thinking or subjective experiences, on which we can base a rational hope and expectation about life after death?

David Watson was an Anglican vicar and a leader of the charismatic renewal in the Church of England. In his late forties he was diagnosed with cancer. In spite of periods of remission the disease progressed until neither he nor those close to him could escape the fact that he was dying.

During his terminal illness he wrote a book recording his thoughts and experiences. It was called *Fear No Evil* (Hodder 1984). Despite having preached and believed the Christian gospel of forgiveness and eternal life for many years, when it came to his own impending death, he wrestled with doubt, as we all do.

His wrestlings, and their conclusion, may help others to reach the same place of assurance and peace that he did:

The big issue

The worst times for me were at two or three o'clock in the morning. I had preached the gospel all over the world with ringing conviction. I had told countless thousands of people that I was not afraid of death since through Christ I had already received God's gift of eternal life. For years I had not doubted these truths at all. But now the most fundamental questions were nagging away insistently, especially in those long hours of the night.

Did Christ really exist? Yes, I had no doubts about that at all. Even Marghanita Laski, a literary critic and self-confessed atheist had told me, 'I find the Gospels totally convincing as historical documents.'

Was Christ really the Son of God? Can he be trusted? He certainly made monstrous and outrageous claims for himself if they were not true. Yet everything in his life, ministry and teaching supported his claims. Here surely was the One Person with the right to speak about all the greatest issues of life and death that puzzle us all. There is every reason why we should trust him.

Did Christ really rise from the dead? Once again, I had for many years sifted through the evidence for this until I was sure beyond any reasonable doubt. The resurrection of Christ was a plain, historical fact – sometimes described as 'the best attested fact in history.' Intellectually, I was as convinced as I possibly could be that Christ had risen from the dead, and this was the solid ground for my own future hopes. Death is not the end. There is life after death.

I am not saying that I never had any problems after that. It would not be true. But in the middle of those nightmare storms, with waves of doubt and fear lashing all around me, I found that my faith was secure on the immovable rock of Christ.

There is only one historical person of whom it is seriously said that he rose from the dead. The founders of other religions are all dead and buried: Abraham in the cave at Hebron, revered by Jews and Muslims alike; the Buddha at various places where his ashes were scattered; Mohammed in the tomb at Medina, the focus of the hajj or pilgrimage that every Muslim is supposed to undertake at least once in a lifetime – to the Prophet's *grave*.

A nation's heroes are buried in state: Napoleon at Les Invalides, Nelson in St Paul's Cathedral in London, Abraham Lincoln in Springfield, Illinois. Charles Darwin and Karl Marx proposed belief systems on which many have based their lives. Great as they all were in their various ways, not one of them is said to have risen from the dead, only Jesus of Nazareth, the 1st century Galilean carpenter–cum-rabbi.

His burial place, much altered as it is, can still be seen in the church of the Holy Sepulchre in Jerusalem, and the tomb is empty, as it was on the first Easter day.

Did Jesus rise from the dead? That is the most momentous question in the world. It is a unique claim, and just because it is a unique claim, it obviously invites scepticism. But, like David Watson, I have studied this claim and I believe that a rigorous examination of the historical facts vindicates it.[2]

It is moreover a claim that has been confirmed by the experience of millions of people throughout the world, starting most famously with the Apostle Paul, people who have met spiritually with Jesus as a living, life-giving, and life-changing presence.

---

[2] The most thorough examinations of the historical evidence for the resurrection of Jesus that I know are to be found in the works of William Lane Craig, e.g. *The Son Rises,* Gipf and Stock, 2001. See also chapter 9.

If it is true that Jesus rose from the dead, the very uniqueness of this event vindicates the claim that Jesus made for himself: that he stood in a unique relationship to God. He was uniquely sent by God to be the Saviour of the world, the God who both made the world and raised Jesus from the dead. It means that uniquely we can trust what Jesus said, about God, about human life and the way to live it, and about life after death.

I endorse all David Watson's conclusions myself, having, like him, fully examined these questions for many years. I have also examined the claims of the other religions of the world and of the atheists, and have come to the same conclusion: that Jesus Christ alone gives me solid ground on which to base my beliefs and hopes about a life after death.

My trust in him has given me a way of life and a set of values with which to live my life here on Earth; a way of life and a set of values very different from those of the world around me, but a way of life and a set of values that in my own life have stood the test of time. It has also given me a sure and certain hope, as sure and certain as any hope can be, that when I die I shall go to be with him, and have everlasting life in a new world, ready to be revealed at the end of time.

Listen to what Jesus said about dying. He said these things to his friends on the night in which he was betrayed, when he knew that he himself was going to die the following day. His purpose was to reassure his followers about the business of dying:

"Do not let your hearts be troubled. Trust in God; trust also in me. In my Father's house are many rooms; if it were not so, I would have told you. I am going there to prepare a place for you. And if I go and prepare a place for you, I will come back and take you to be with me that you also may be where I am. You know the way to the place where I am going."

Thomas said to him, "Lord, we don't know where you are going, so how can we know the way?" Jesus answered, "I am the way and the truth and the life. No-one comes to the Father except through me." **John 14:1-6**

This faith puts a completely different complexion on the years of retirement and the prospect of dying.

If you do not already share this faith, but want to examine the questions involved as David Watson did and as I have done, I recommend that you find a church that runs the *Alpha Course*, the best introduction that I know to the Christian faith, and a chance to explore the meaning of life and death. With this faith I can face the challenges of retirement and old age with hope rather than despair.

Whatever the trials of old age may be, I can look forward in the hope that the best is yet to be. Although many of my life's experiences are now in the past, my best days are not behind but ahead of me, and I can look towards the future with a lively expectation.

I can enjoy the pleasures of old age, of children and grandchildren, of a rest and relaxation that the pressures of work so often denied me; I can eat, drink and be merry, not because tomorrow I die, but because tomorrow I live.

This faith also gives me a purpose with which to fill the years of my retirement: to go on serving the God and Father of our Lord Jesus Christ in whatever way I can, until he calls me home.

Having come to terms with my own mortality, I can plan my remaining years on earth to be as fruitful and worthwhile as possible for Christ and his Kingdom, until he receives me into glory.

Chapter Three

WHAT ARE YOU GOING TO DO ALL DAY?

'Retirement is a full-time occupation,' said a friend. 'You are retired twenty-four hours a day. It is a big job.'

That is perhaps the best starting point from which to approach retirement. It is a major milestone along life's way, and the beginning of a very different way of life. By the time we reach retirement, we have already experienced and negotiated many such life-changing moments: leaving school, marrying, having children, the same children growing up and leaving home, and now retirement, the end of our working lives. It is always difficult to prepare for these changes in life; we only really learn how to do new things by actually doing them.

Part of the difficulty of approaching the milestone of retirement is that we tend to look forward to it in terms of holidays.

What are you going to do all day?

For the past forty years we have looked forward, perhaps from one year's end to the next, to our annual holidays: times to relax, to please ourselves, to pursue a personal interest or hobby, to travel, to fulfil other ambitions, to spend more time with our spouses or families. Now, in retirement, life will be one long holiday. What could be better than that?

But it is salutary to look at retirement from another point of view. Retirement is another word for unemployment, and most of our lives we have lived with the thought that nothing could be worse than that.

For the past forty years we may have dreaded the possibility of being made redundant – now we are going to be made redundant for the rest of our lives. There is a whole industry built up around helping those who have been made redundant: retraining, job seeking, and counselling for the long-term unemployed. But here we are, facing retirement, and that means facing permanent unemployment – a much more daunting prospect than a permanent holiday, and surprisingly there is no industry to help us with it.

This highlights the ambiguity of our present practice of retirement, which is, after all, fairly recent. Only with the introduction of the universal old-age pension has the prospect of retirement been a realistic one for most of the population. Until then, people had to work until they dropped in order to support themselves, and if they became unable to work, there was only the goodness of their families or the 'relief' of the Workhouse to fall back on, and many people saw the Workhouse as a fate worse than death.

At a time when so much of the world's work was heavy manual work of one sort or another, it is not surprising that few people lived beyond seventy. There is no doubt that the opportunity of retirement on a pension has lightened the burden of toil and lengthened the span of life for many.

As we grow older, usually somewhere around the age of sixty, there is no doubt that we become tired more quickly, and that many of our faculties begin to deteriorate. So from the point of view of the employer as well as that of the employee, it is clear that some adjustment in the nature and the pattern of work for a person in their sixties is desirable.

What are you going to do all day?

It is much less clear that our present practice of working a full forty-hour week up to the day that we turn sixty-five (or whatever the statutory retiring age may be), and then suddenly not working at all, is a sensible practice from anybody's point of view. From the employer's and the economy's point of view much valuable experience and expertise is arbitrarily consigned to the scrap heap, and from the employee's point of view, he or she suffers a sudden and violent disruption to their lives.

It seems a pity that society, and the various trades and professions, cannot devise a gentler and more gradual system of retirement, a change of roles within the workplace or a more gradual winding-down, that enables a smoother and more productive transition to be made.

One of the advantages of self-employment may be that you can give yourself the chance to manage your retirement more gradually. But most of us live in a world in which the system dictates a sharp and sudden change, from employment to unemployment, and so we have to prepare ourselves and manage it as best we can.

The best is yet to be

Through all the changing scenes of life, the secret of happiness is to look forward and not back. Every time of life has its own pleasures and opportunities, just as every time of life has its own challenges and struggles.

We may look back nostalgically on the days of our youth or the days when our children were young, but each of those ages had its trials and tribulations as well. We tend to forget the agonies of unrequited teenage love, and the sleepless nights with crying babies.

Living a happy and fulfilled life means making the most of the opportunities and pleasures that each stage of life brings and at the same time facing and overcoming its particular challenges. Retirement is no different. It has some of the pleasures of a permanent holiday and some of the struggles of permanent unemployment. The balance between the two will depend a good deal on how we used to feel about our work.

For some people, their career has been the means of their personal fulfilment. They loved their work, getting up on a Monday morning with a song in their hearts and a spring in their steps.

That does not mean that there are not elements of drudgery in every occupation, nor that in everyone's work there are not times and situations of difficulty or hardship. But for some, their work has been a source of profound satisfaction and joy.

The satisfaction may have been in making things, or in serving their fellow human beings. But in one way or another they have been able to use the gifts that God has given them and they have found their identity in what they did. For such as these, retirement is a profound loss.

Bertram, for example, had been a leading plastic surgeon. He had worked his way up the medical ladder until he was at the very top, one of only five such specialists in the country. He found retirement very hard: 'No one needs me anymore,' he said.

Others have gone through life, if not hating, at least only tolerating their work. It is a tragic way to live a life. My advice to young people learning or training and looking forward to career choices, has always been: 'Find something to do that you enjoy doing. It does not matter how much you get paid for it, but life is too short to spend it doing something you hate.'

Some people, however, through financial necessity or lack of opportunity, have had to do just that. Tom spent his life working as a farm labourer. He always wanted to be a carpenter or cabinet-maker, but he never had the opportunity to learn the craft or trade.

For people like this, retirement seems like release after a life-sentence. But even prisoners, especially those who have served long sentences, find release and life in the outside world a very difficult adjustment to make. Everyone, in different ways, can feel disorientated and lost when suddenly deprived of the support and the familiarity of the routines and responsibilities of work.

So, what are you going to do all day? It is the question that faces you on the first morning after your retirement. You may have a hangover from your retirement party, and your first thought may be to stay in bed. But beware of the lure of the lie-in. Staying in bed is not a solution to the problem of what to do all day.

36

What are you going to do all day?

Get up, even if you are not sure what to get up for. One lie-in a week is said to be healthy, but otherwise not getting up is the first step to giving up.

For as long as we can remember, people have had expectations of us. From early childhood we were expected to get up and go to school. Since whenever our education finished and we started work, we have been expected to be at the office or the factory at a certain hour, and during our time there we have been expected to perform certain duties and to achieve certain results.

Even the woman who has stayed at home has been the subject of expectations: her babies, her children and her husband have expected to be fed, have expected to have clean clothes to put on and a clean house to live in.

Today, on the first day of retirement, nobody has any expectations of you. The big change in your life is that now nobody is going to fill your time for you: you have to fill your time for yourself. 'Retirement is a full-time occupation; you are retired twenty-four hours a day. It is a big job.' Where do we start?

Again, we need to begin with the bigger issue: this time, purpose. What is the meaning of life? What is the purpose of living?

Retirement books and retirement courses often urge us to take up new hobbies or pastimes, to do all those things that we have always wanted to do but for which we have never had the time. This begs the question: why have we spent our lives doing things that we did not want to do and why have we not found time to do the things that we did want to do?

There seems to be a very sad assumption behind this advice: that we have been forced by circumstances to spend the previous forty or fifty years doing things that we, at best tolerated, at worst hated. If that is true, it is sad indeed, and retirement may then be a wonderful opportunity to do something more congenial. If it is not true, we have the greater problem of losing the very thing that gave us happiness and fulfilment and replacing it with something else.

Either way, hobbies and pastimes are not a substitute for purpose. There is something desperate about the idea of pastimes. During our years of employment we should have found ways of relaxing and turning our minds away from the preoccupations and pressures of work. These may well be called hobbies: golf, football, collecting stamps, going to the pub, playing bridge, singing in a choir, bird-watching, keeping ferrets, gardening. But they scarcely constitute a reason for living.

Time is not something merely to be passed, unless we are waiting for a train. Time, like money, is something to be spent carefully and wisely. We are given a limited supply of both time and money in this world, and it is irresponsible and foolish to fritter them away either in pointless expenditure or prodigal waste. Both time and money should be used for some good purpose.

But what purpose?

Is there any purpose to life? This is another of the big issues that retirement forces us to face. Many people are afflicted by a sense of the ultimate futility of all that they do, even those in full-time work.

It is the sense of futility expressed by Macbeth in Shakespeare's play:

The best is yet to be

Tomorrow, and tomorrow, and tomorrow,
Creeps in this petty pace from day to day,
To the last syllable of recorded time;
And all our yesterdays have lighted fools
The way to dusty death. Out, out, brief candle!
Life's but a walking shadow, a poor player,
That struts and frets his hour upon the stage,
And then is heard no more; it is a tale
Told by an idiot, full of sound and fury,
Signifying nothing.

Life as well as literature is full of examples of such tragic despair. Bob Jones was a golfer who in 1930 won all four major US/British tournaments in the same year. He went on to become an engineer, a writer, a lawyer and a film-maker.

In his mid-forties he contracted a rare disease of the spinal column which led to a creeping paralysis. He died aged seventy. He had come from a prosperous background and was described at his funeral as 'a Southern gentleman.'

One way and another Bob Jones had experienced almost everything that life has to offer: wealth, fame, success, a variety of occupations and fields of achievement, as well as suffering and pain. Yet his last words were, 'Is that all there is to it?'

In a similar vein the British comic actor Kenneth Williams wrote in the last entry in his diary, 'Oh, what's the bloody point.' He died the same day of an overdose of drugs.

So what is the point? This brings us back, whether we like it or not, to the Big Issue that we discussed in the first chapter: is there anything beyond this life and this world.

If not, if all that we have is this material universe and this flesh and blood, then ultimately there is no point or purpose in life. One day we shall all be gone and the universe itself will be cold and dead, and it will be as though we had never been. In that case it does not finally matter what any of us do; life itself is only a pastime, passing the time as best we can between birth and death.

But suppose that there is more to it than that. Suppose that there is a God, who made the universe and placed us here for a purpose. Suppose that there is the possibility of life after death, that death is not the end, but that we shall be judged in some way for the things that we have done, that we are accountable for the use that we make of the days that are allotted to us here on earth.

The 17th century Shorter Catechism posed the question: 'What is the chief end of man?' To which the reply was: 'To glorify God and to enjoy him forever.' We glorify God not only with our lips but with our lives, and for a believer that gives life a meaning and a purpose - a purpose that informs everything that we do, not least in retirement.

There are as many ways of enjoying God and glorifying him in retirement as there are at any other times in our lives, though they may be different ways.

Paul the Apostle tells us 'to make the most of every opportunity, because the days are evil' (Ephesians 5:16). The world is full of need and misery of one sort or another, and no-one is exempt, whatever their age, from the responsibility of making the world a better place.

People are perishing throughout the world for want of the basic necessities of life: food and shelter, education and love. Even in retirement it is still possible to make a difference, to contribute even in small ways to making the world a better place.

No less, people are perishing for want of a sense of meaning and purpose in life, and no follower of Jesus is exempt from making him known as the Saviour of the world. Even in retirement it is still possible to be part of that great commission to make Jesus known, to our neighbours as much as to those at the ends of the earth.

How each one of us works out these responsibilities depends on our gifts, our abilities, and our opportunities. But retirement is not an excuse to opt out of them. It is an opportunity to develop new gifts and abilities, or to discover new ways of using those that we already have, in the service of God and of our fellow human beings.

So, the first job in retirement is to reappraise the sum of our gifts and abilities. Please God, some of those gifts and abilities may have been used already, developed and refined in the jobs we have done and the training that we have received. Others may, up until now, have been dormant and unused.

43

Retirement is an opportunity to make the most of those gifts, whatever they are, free from the necessity of earning a living. An old age pension, whether from the state or from an employer, is an extraordinary grace: money that is given to us that we no longer have to earn. But it is not an excuse for living in idleness.

We are still taking up space on this planet and using up its resources. We ought also to be making some contribution to it and to those with whom we share it. Living on a pension is no different in principle to living on any other sort of benefit; if we contribute nothing to society in return, we are no better than spongers.

So, quite simply, what can I do? What have I learnt to do? What am I gifted to do? What do I want to do?

In my own case, I spent my life as an Anglican clergyman. I was called by God in my youth and, with all the provisos mentioned above, I have enjoyed my life and my calling and I arrived at the age of retirement with a sense of thankfulness and satisfaction, and with no regrets about the course my life had taken.

What are you going to do all day?

I have discovered that my gifts, such as they are, lie primarily in the use of words. I cannot draw or paint; I love singing but I cannot play a musical instrument to my own, let alone anybody else's satisfaction. I also discovered at school that I was a born leader rather than a follower, not with a huge amount of physical courage, but with the courage to step out into new ventures and surmount the obstacles that I encountered.

At the age of sixty-five, I was glad to relinquish the responsibilities and burdens of church leadership, but at the same time I lost the opportunities that church leadership had given me to make use of these gifts. But I had started to write during the years when I was still employed as a vicar, and it became a natural transition to writing as, more or less, a second career.

I was called to be a minister of the Word, and now that I no longer have the same opportunities to preach and teach in the congregation, I have found a way to go on fulfilling my calling through writing books like this one. I have continued in retirement to use the gifts that I have used all my life, but in a different way.

By contrast, retirement for others may mean the discovery of gifts that were previously unused, perhaps even unknown. Retirement is an opportunity to try something new. As with the choices that a young person should make, consult your heart. What do you want to do?

Retirement is this wonderful chance to do what you want to do, rather than doing what you have had to do to make ends meet. Do not waste the chance by doing nothing. There are many opportunities today even for older people to pursue education and training: classes, courses, at colleges, institutes, the Open University. Try it, whatever it is. Search the public library, the internet, prospectuses, until you find someone somewhere to give you the new skills or new knowledge that you want.

I cannot do the work of appraising your gifts and abilities for you or for anyone else. Each one of us must do that work for ourselves: identifying the gifts we may have already used or discovering the gifts that may until now have lain unused. But I am sure that God has given everyone gifts and that, if we ask, he will give us the discernment to see what they are, and the grace to use them in his service.

Once we have identified our gifts, the next question is, how can we use them in retirement? There may be ways in which you can go on using your gifts in some part-time employment. Many companies today rely as much on part-time as on full-time employees.

You may be able to offer your skills on a free-lance basis, as a consultant or an advisor or a trainer. George Bernard Shaw said, 'Those who can, do; those who can't, teach.' It was a cynical remark, but it may contain a seed of hope for the retired. If the reason that you cannot 'do' any more is that you are retired, then perhaps you can teach others to do it instead.

Brian had worked all his life as an engineer. In retirement he found a useful and positive occupation teaching numeracy on a part-time basis in the local prison. For the more adventurous there are even opportunities, through organisations like VSO, for healthy, retired people to go abroad to teach or advise in developing countries.

The best is yet to be

There are almost unlimited opportunities to be useful in an unpaid capacity. There are local councils and quangos, boards of school and hospital governors, to which you can apply for appointment or election. In Britain, there is a long tradition of involving 'lay-people' in the process of governance, from serving as Justices of the Peace to serving on village hall management committees. Churches and charities are largely dependent on volunteers.

Retired people are an invaluable source of volunteer help. There is a national network of centres that exist to link up volunteers with organisations that want volunteer help. You can find out about these centres and the opportunities they offer at www.do-it.org.uk.

If you see a social need on your doorstep, there is almost certainly a local church or charity that has a programme to meet it, and if not, then why not start one? A healthy society is one in which local citizens are actively involved in it.

At his Inauguration as President of the United States, John F. Kennedy said, 'Ask not what your country can do for you; ask what you can do for your country.' Or, if that sounds too grandiloquent, then ask not what your neighbours can do for you; ask what you can do for your neighbours.

Mike retired to the country after a career in the Metropolitan Police. Having dealt with battered women from a policeman's point of view, Mike became a founding trustee and chairman of a project providing a safe house and help for victims of domestic violence.

He became involved in the regional Mental Health Partnership NHS Trust eventually acting as chairman of that also. He threw himself into the activities of the local Village Hall Committee and also volunteered as a carer with the Home Hospice scheme. He served a term as churchwarden of his church.

These activities were spread out over a period of some fifteen to twenty years but Mike made good use of his time and talents to continue serving the communities in which he now found himself. He put to use the experience of his working life and the abilities that he had acquired there, as well as discovering new ways of serving others.

The best is yet to be

For Mike, retirement did not mean idleness, but a chance to take stock of where he was and what he could do in this new phase of his life.

The church to which I belong relies on retired people to perform the following tasks, amongst others: a retired horticulturalist to be a church-warden; a retired solicitor's secretary to take the minutes of the Church Council; a retired bank-manager to keep the books; a retired builder to manage the premises; a retired couple as sacristans; a retired civil servant as caretaker; retired people, amongst others, to welcome worshippers, make coffee, copy the CDs; and me, to preach occasionally.

This task of taking stock and exploring a new landscape is not one that can be completed within a couple of weeks of finishing work. Most retired people find that a new pattern of life takes months or even years to emerge. After all, few people have had the opportunity to give the matter much time or thought until the day after they retired.

Up until then we still had to go to work; we still had jobs to do. So most of us are starting from scratch the day after we retire, and worse than that the problem itself has probably caught us unawares.

So, give yourself time to build up alternative ways of filling the hours. Do not rush at it like a bull at a gate; pick up new threads one at a time. That may mean enduring days of emptiness and a feeling of disorientation. But provided we do not give up, a new life will emerge, and it may be a life that contains some wonderful surprises.

It is probably the case that we shall have to take the initiative ourselves. Sometimes a retired person may be approached by others and asked to take on some new responsibility or task in either a voluntary or paid capacity. If that happens we need to think carefully before saying yes. The prospect of being needed again may seem to offer a welcome relief from the apparent aimlessness of retirement, but we do not want to be released from one form of captivity, only to enter into another.

In any case, it is more likely that if we want to develop a new interest or find a new occupation in retirement the initiative is going to have to be our own. Gone are the days when people are coming knocking at our door, if ever they did.

51

We are going to have to go out and knock on theirs. In that respect finding things to do in retirement is like finding a new job after we have been made redundant. But just as we do not expect the unemployed to sit around waiting for employers to come looking for them, so, if we, the retired, want some useful and satisfying occupation we will have, in a famous phrase, to 'get on our bikes' and go out looking for them.

But when all is said and done, we are supposed to be slowing down in our old age. Some retired people panic at the prospect of having nothing to do all day. They rush about filling up their time so that, as they say to you with a smug smile, 'I am so busy I do not know how I found time to go to work.'

Those people have missed the point of retirement, which is to relax, do less, reflect more, and let the pressures of life fall away. Keep up the hobbies or pastimes that you have enjoyed in the past, and maybe discover new ones.

Rest is not a sin. Indeed it is a commandment that is too much ignored in today's frantic whirl of getting and spending. Many people's lives do not allow them the amount of time that they need to rest. Retirement is a time to put that right and, as all the politicians say when they have been sacked or voted out of office: it is an opportunity to spend more time with the family.

The first member of your family with whom you will have more time to spend is your wife or your husband, assuming that you have one. (If you don't, then you can skip the next bit) But for both of you, retirement may come as something of a shock to your relationship. Whatever you have both been doing for the last forty years, whether you have both been working or whether one of you has been keeping the house, you will both have formed habits independently of each other.

So, retirement may be similar to the time when you were first married. Then, you had come from different families and households where things were done differently, and you had to adjust your lives to each other's ways and make new habits and arrangements that were acceptable to you both. Retirement may mean similar adjustments.

All their married life Tony had been going out to work every day from 8.30 to 5.00 and Dot had

53

had the house to herself. When Tony retired he was about the house all day. He was generally busy with his own activities, but Dot felt that she had lost her own space. For Tony and Dot the solution was to turn one of the spare bedrooms into a workroom or studio for Tony so that each of them could do their own things without being on top of one other.

But retirement is also an opportunity to do more things together, to spend more time together. When you first met, presumably there were interests that you had in common, things that you enjoyed doing together: going out to the cinema or the theatre, going for walks in the country, listening to music, having meals together.

Much of that had to stop when the first child came along, and work may have left one or both of you too tired to make the effort in recent years. But now you can pick up the threads of your life together as a couple, and enjoy the sort of togetherness that only forty years of sharing life's joys and sorrows together can bring.

There is also of course the possibility that you have drifted apart or even become seriously estranged in the preceding years. In which case there is now the time to address these issues that perhaps there has not been before: hours, rather than minutes in which to talk to one another.

If you are out of practice, or were never in practice at talking to one another about your feelings, you may find this a difficult exercise. I suggest that you find help. Only the two of you can sort out your hurts and differences, but other people can offer you encouragement and techniques for communicating with one another. It is not too late in middle or old age to take a course like *The Marriage Course*.

The Marriage Course is another resource, like the *Alpha Course* mentioned in the previous chapter, that many churches offer, in this case to those wishing to improve their marriages. If there are strains in your relationship, the onset of retirement may make them worse, but it also offers an opportunity not to be missed to resolve these issues.

The alternative is to endure your remaining years together in a state of hostility or armed neutrality, all the more uncomfortable because you are now in so much closer proximity and

55

spending so much more time in each other's company. How much more worthwhile then to make the effort to find peace and reconciliation, and to re-find the love that you had for one another at the beginning. It is still there. You need only to clear away the debris of unhealed wounds and unresolved quarrels that have blighted your relationship since then. The secret is to talk.

Finally, retirement is an opportunity to spend more time with God. You may never have taken God seriously, or seriously enough. Our middle years are often so full of work, of raising children, of leisure pursuits, of getting and spending, that we ignore God.

Even if we have an underlying disposition to believe, we have never got around to going to church. Retirement is an opportunity to put all that right. God is a serious matter, whether we believe in him or not.

Everyone needs to think seriously about the ultimate questions of life, and at least come to a considered opinion about them. They are too important, too much is at stake, to brush them aside forever.

If you have a vague or half-formed faith, then now is the time to firm or sharpen it up. I have already mentioned the *Alpha Course* twice, and I will mention it again: I know no better way to think through the meaning of life and the basics of the Christian faith.

If your faith is already clear and settled, then retirement offers the chance to spend more time in reading and studying the Bible, more time in prayer, and more time in the fellowship of the church.

It is impossible to put a worldly value on the contribution that many older Christians make to the life of the church, the nation and the world by their prayers. Such service is largely secret and invisible, known only to God but, I believe, precious and powerful in his sight. The last spiritual revival in Britain took place in the Hebridean Islands in 1948. It is commonly traced to the fervent prayers of two old women, blind Peggy and her arthritic sister Christine.

In Hinduism, the ideal life consists of four stages: *brahmacarya*, the life of discipline and education; *garhasthya,* the life of the householder and worker; *vanaprasthya,* the loosening of the bonds; and *sannyasa*, the life of the hermit.

Nothing in Christianity suggests that the life of the hermit is anything more than a rare and special vocation; Christianity values love above all things, not only the love of God but also the love of one another, and Christians marry until death us do part. But there is a wisdom in the Hindu philosophy: old age and retirement are a time for more meditation, meditation on life, meditation on our experience, and meditation on God.

There is an old joke about a little girl who saw her grandmother reading her Bible and warned her friend not to make a noise: 'Granny is studying for her finals,' she whispered. It should not be a joke. We should be studying for our finals, not because we are worried about passing, but because we should be preparing for the life of the world to come.

Chapter Four

THE ART OF
GRAND-PARENTING

We were not made by God to be solitary individuals. For most people, going to work meant much more than earning a living. The office or the factory, the school or the hospital, was a place where we belonged. We made friends there; we were known; if we were absent, we were missed.

Working together creates community, and the place of work was one of the principle communities to which we belonged. Retirement therefore means much more than simply getting our money without having to earn it. It means exclusion from that old community of work.

There is nothing sadder than going back to the place where you once worked after you have retired. There they all are, still working together, but you are now an outsider, and no amount of chat about the old days or about how old so-and-so is getting on, can disguise the fact that you no longer belong there. One of the principle questions to face us in retirement is, where do I belong?

When God made Adam, his first observation about him was that it was not good for the man to be alone (Genesis 2:18). Adam had God as a constant spiritual companion, but God saw that that was not enough. Adam needed another human helper to be with him. So, God created Eve. God's primary remedy for our need for belonging is the family.

Under the Old Covenant the People of God were defined as a family: the descendents of Abraham, Isaac and Jacob. Jewishness is conveyed by the blood-line. So, Judaism is essentially a family religion. The primary responsibility for teaching the faith to the next generation lies not with preachers or rabbis but with parents. The Lord says, 'Teach these words of mine to your children, talking about them when you sit at home and when you walk along the road, when you lie down and when you get up' (Deuteronomy 11:19).

Jewish celebrations and festivals are family ones. The celebration of the Sabbath takes place in the home on Friday evening. The celebration of the Passover is a family meal (Exodus 12:3). While the temple, and later the synagogue, brought together the wider Jewish community, the focus of the faith has always been in the home.

The coming of Jesus, the Messiah, rewrote the terms of the Covenant between God and his People in many ways. Not the least of these ways, and not the least offensive no doubt to contemporary Jewish sensibilities, was that Jesus declared that his coming would disrupt this family solidarity: that loyalty to him would henceforth be more important than loyalty to the family (Matthew 10:35-38).

With the coming of Jesus, membership of the People of God is no longer defined by blood or natural descent, but by faith in him (John 1:13). So, the family in Christianity does not have the same centrality that it does in Judaism.

The church, as the family of God, assumes that central role in the life of the followers of Jesus. The church is the essential place where the faith is taught and where the feasts and commemorations are celebrated. Nevertheless, Jesus does not abolish the family as the creation ordinance of God. On the contrary he affirms it (Matthew 19:4-6) and he takes care to provide for his own family (John 19:26-27).

While it is clear from the book of Acts and the letters of Paul that conversion to Christ often splits families, Christians are to persevere and pray for the salvation of their partners, and to bring up their children in the training and instruction of the Lord.

While the church can and will fill the place of families in supporting Christian widows and orphans, this is still the primary responsibility of blood relations, if they exist. The natural obligations of family life are not superseded or made redundant by conversion to Christ (1 Timothy 5:4). The ideal remains the natural family, united in faith in Christ, passing on the faith from one generation to another and supporting one another from birth to death.

The natural family, within or alongside the church, is still a place of belonging that endures, irrespective of our faith or of our ages. The family is, or should be, a source of mutual support at every stage of our lives, whether its members are Christians or not. It is a vital support for children and it becomes an ever more important source of help as we get older, and retirement is indeed a chance to spend more time with the family.

From here on in this chapter, I have to assume that you have such a family, that you have children and that you now have or are about to have grandchildren. If you have been single or childless, you will have to adapt the contents of this chapter about the art of grand-parenting to the art of being an uncle or an aunt, a godparent or a friend of the family. But in any case I do recommend that you have children somewhere in your life.

One of the greatest joys throughout my own life has been to be a member of a church. The church is, or should be, a family of people of all ages. As a child in a church in London, I had many adults in my life outside the circle of my blood relations who were friends, who talked to me, taught me, encouraged me, and widened my experience of people and their lives. As one of the older generation, I now rejoice in belonging to a church in which I have many young friends, from toddlers to teenagers, who talk to me, whom I sometimes teach, whom I can encourage and who still widen my experience of people and life.

I love the church as an inter-generational community of God's people, and, particularly if you are childless, the church provides a unique way to enjoy the company and friendship of children, and to be a blessing to them as they can be to you. Jesus loved children, and there is something sad about us if we do not do the same.

But if, in addition to the children of the church family, we do have children and grandchildren of our own, then we have a unique role to play in their lives as grandparents. This will be for us a new and different role in the family, one that we have not played before and one that involves some major adjustments and a lot of new learning. Being a grandparent is not just picking up the threads of parenting where we left off. Grand-parenting is an altogether different art.

Perhaps we need first to look at what grandparents do not do: they do not try to be parents again. Everyone parents their own children in a different way and none of us are perfect parents. Please God, when we were parents we did some things right, but it is certain that we also did some things wrong. Our children survived our parenting, and we hope that they flourished under it; but they will not parent their own children in exactly the same way as we parented them. All sorts of things have changed for them.

The world around us has changed. Fashions in parenting have changed. Not so long ago the book of Proverbs provided a model for parenting: 'Spare the rod and spoil the child' (Proverbs 13:24, mediated through Samuel Butler). That fashion has changed: today there is a very strong social, if not legal, taboo on hitting children at all.

No one would condone the Dickensian excesses of cruelty and sadism that this biblical saying was sometimes used to justify, both at home and at school in days gone by, but the pendulum has now swung, as pendulums do, to the opposite extreme: teachers are afraid even to touch children in school.

When they were small, my wife and I smacked our children on the bottom if they were deliberately disobedient. I do not believe that it did them any damage, physical or mental, and I think that it was effective as a discipline in a way that trying to reason with a two or three year old may not be. They learnt their lessons. One of our two children now smacks his children in a similar way; our daughter does not believe in corporal punishment at all.

It is not for us, as grandparents to comment on their views and practices: they both love their children and want the best for them. Those children will survive and flourish even though they are growing up under different regimes. As grandparents we need to honour their parents' decisions rather than to criticize them or try to impose views of our own.

Not only has the world changed, but our child is only one half of a couple that now have the responsibility of bringing up their children together. These two people, the mother and the father, have come from different families which did things in different ways, from how they celebrated Christmas to how they scrambled eggs. Marriage is a process of discovering and adapting to those differences. It is the necessary process of give and take, and it applies to the upbringing of children.

A couple may have brought to the marriage very different expectations about children's bedtimes, about feeding, about diet, about television-time, about what is safe and what is harmful. It is not a good idea for grandparents to interfere in this process of negotiation between husband and wife; they have to work things out for themselves.

Either separately or together, they will be reacting to their own experiences of being parented. Some of the ways we followed, they may choose to follow too; on the other hand, some of our ways they may want to reject. It is their right and their responsibility to do it their way, not ours.

It is sometimes a hard lesson for us grandparents to learn, that the discipline of our grandchildren and making decisions about them is not our job. We may disagree with some of the decisions that our children make about their children: where to send them to school, what other activities to allow or encourage, how much freedom to give them as they grow up.

We may not approve of the way our grandchildren behave, and are perhaps allowed to behave by their parents, but for the most part our job is to keep quiet and leave these matters to their parents.

If the grandchildren are left in our sole care either for an hour or for a week, then we have to use our own discretion. For their parents' sake, as much as our own and theirs, we cannot let them run wild. But we have to reinforce the regime and discipline of their parents, and back up the decisions that their parents have made: 'Mummy and Daddy would not let you do that, would they?' or 'Daddy and Mummy think that that is best for you.'

It is not generally the role of grandparents to interfere in the upbringing of their grandchildren but to encourage and support their children in what we have all found, in our own generations, to be a difficult and demanding job.

Grandparents can of course be guilty of the opposite fault: not of being too strict with their grandchildren, but of spoiling them and encouraging them or letting them get away with things that their parents would never allow.

That brings us to the thorny issue of grandparental jealousy. Grandparents are in a unique relationship to the rest of the family. On the one hand, we have a privileged access to the lives and loves of our children and grandchildren.

By welcoming us into their homes from the first days of their children's lives, our children convey to their own children that we are people who are special, people who can be trusted and who belong to them, in a way that no other adults besides themselves do. At the same time, we are not part of their immediate family; we remain for many purposes outsiders, and we have to be content with that privileged but limited role.

There is a temptation to curry favour with our grandchildren, encouraging cupboard love, showering them with sweets and presents as a way of buying their affection and enticing them into wanting to spend time with us. There can even be an undertone of competition with the parents themselves for the love of our grandchildren.

Then there are the in-law grandparents. We may feel ourselves to be in competition with them, to be the most beloved grandparents; anything they can give, we can give better.

All these forms of jealousy and competition are likely to prove disruptive and unhelpful to the well-being of our children and their families. Let us glory in the unique and privileged place we have in the lives of our grandchildren, while resisting the temptation to assume or covet a place that is not our own. We are allowed to have a share in the lives of these little people, but it is a small share – and we must learn to be grateful and content with that.

If we learn to accept these boundaries then we can be a source of great blessing to both parents and children. We have things to give our grandchildren that perhaps their parents cannot give.

The first of these is time. Parents are busy people. Today both parents probably have jobs outside the home, and those jobs may be very demanding of their time and energy. When they get home they still have to do all the work of keeping house and looking after the children: cooking, cleaning, shopping, washing, gardening, mending, and paying the bills, as well as trying to squeeze in time for lives of their own as individuals and as a couple. How much time and energy do they have left over to play with the children, read them books, help them with their homework, take them out, and, above all, listen to them?

Much of the work that parents used to do for their children, caring for them, educating them, and entertaining them, is now delegated to child-minders. teachers and the television, but grandparents may have a valuable role also. Grandparents have something that parents often do not have: time, perhaps too much time, on their hands.

What better way to spend some of our time than on our grandchildren. If we live near to them, we can be free baby-sitters, available to pick up the children from school, to provide cover in times of sickness. If we live further away, we can have the grandchildren for holidays. We may have interests or hobbies that we can share with our grandchildren, opening doors for them into activities and worlds that perhaps they might otherwise never enter or know.

We can take them to places of interest or excitement, not just children's playgrounds or pleasure parks, but theatres, sporting events, to see the Changing of the Guard at Buckingham Palace or the Edinburgh Tattoo. This is not instead of whatever their parents might do, but in addition to those things. We grandparents after all may have more time, and perhaps more money, to spend on these children than their hard-pressed, working parents.

Above all, we have time to talk to them and to listen to them, to play games at the table with them and to read them books, to hear about what they have been doing, and to answer their questions.

There may be circumstances in which we are called upon to play a larger role in our grandchildren's lives. The arrival of new baby may mean that grandma is called upon to go and run the family home while Mum is in hospital, or to have the older siblings to stay at her house. Parental separation or divorce may mean that the children need a lot of extra love, support, and reassurance that the whole world is not falling apart around them. Grandparents can at such times be a much-needed source of continuing stability and security.

Grandparents can sometimes be called upon to be either short-term or long-term child-minders or carers for their grandchildren. But we should think carefully before we allow these demands to escalate. Parenting, as God has arranged it, is a job for young people, and for good reason.

Young children make a lot of demands on our energy, and parenting teenagers can be an emotionally stressful business. Are we fit and strong enough to bear these burdens and responsibilities in our old age?

It may be the best of a bad job or an inescapable obligation, but we need seriously to weigh the implications. Many children who have suffered the trauma of parental loss have been blessed by grandparents who took them in, loved them and brought them up. But such obligations, like those of marriage itself, should not be 'enterprised, nor taken in hand, unadvisedly, lightly or wantonly, but reverently, discreetly, advisedly, soberly and in the fear of God.'

In any case, all these interventions, from the greatest to the least, should be seen as a matter of us grandparents *offering* not pushing ourselves forward, offering our time and our help, prepared and content to be refused as well as accepted.

The second resource that grandparents have to offer is experience. Can any generation learn from the experience of previous ones? It is a moot point. It seems too often, in everything from politics to playing with matches, that every generation has to make its own mistakes and learn its own lessons the hard way.

George Santayana wrote, 'Those who do not learn from history are doomed to repeat it.' We do spend most of our time repeating our ancestors' mistakes. Yet we can but try to teach the next generation the lessons that we have learned in our own.

Simply telling our grandchildren stories of our own childhood gives them a sense of the world before they were born and the continuity of the generations. The current popular vogue for tracing ancestors and drawing up family trees is a sign that people have a need for a sense of their personal roots and origins, a need that was once satisfied orally by stories told by grandparents of themselves and of their own parents and grandparents.

From this source alone I can tell my grandchildren about their family history going back to 1838 and the lives of my own great-grandfathers, one a cobbler in Lympstone near Exeter and the other a Bible Christians minister in Shebbear, also in Devon.

But with families living ever further away from one another in this mobile age, we are increasingly cut off from such roots and from the sources of information about who we are and where we have come from. Provided that grandparents do not indulge themselves too liberally in reminiscences about 'the good old days', they can give their grandchildren that valuable sense of belonging to a succession of generations spanning the years.

Just as valuable, though to be dispensed in equally small doses, is the advice that we can give our grandchildren after some sixty or seventy years spent on this Earth, years during which we have lived through and survived for better or worse all the experiences that are now and will be theirs.

The older generation today is often confused by the rapid advance of technology, the internet, computer games, mobile phones, texts, apps, blogs, and tweets, and hence intimidated into thinking that their own experience of life is worth nothing in this new electronic age. But the fundamentals of human life, and above all the fundamental that is God, do not change; technology is merely a veneer.

What is underneath in the hearts and minds of men and women and in the loving purposes of God remains the same. Our human needs, of love, of meaning and purpose, and of God, are always the same.

Psalm 119 is full of a sense of gratitude and love for God's law, his word and his testimony, his commandments and his statutes. To many people it might seem odd to love God's law; we are more likely to feel it as a burden and a constraint, to be accepted, at best, reluctantly but with as good a grace as we can muster. But God's law is simply God's advice to us, the human beings that he has made, about how to live our lives in a way that will bring us joy and fulfillment.

For a truly happy and complete life it is best to love God and to love one another, not to kill, steal, commit adultery, lie or covet what God has given to other people. God is only concerned that we should get the best out of life and avoid the mistakes that all too easily spoil or destroy our lives and the lives of others.

Our own view of life is often too small and too narrow. We quickly lose sight of the bigger picture, of our place in God's purposes and of the span of the existence that he has planned for us, even eternity.

It was this that brought about our downfall at the beginning. Adam and Eve were given Paradise to live in, and eternity to enjoy it. But it all depended on one condition: obedience to God. Confronted with the forbidden fruit Eve chose five minutes of taste sensation over the joys of an endless future beyond it. She and Adam lost both Paradise and eternity for the sake of an all-too-transient pleasure.

All too often we make the same mistake. We are all vulnerable to the temptations of short-term gratification at the expense of longer-term happiness. Presented with a plate of roast potatoes and Brussels sprouts most children will eat the potatoes first and the sprouts second. To develop the self-discipline of delayed gratification, to eat the things we don't like before the things that we do, is mark of maturity, but a maturity that some people never achieve. But the principle is of a wider application: we need to see our lives as a whole, to resist the things that may look attractive in the present moment but which will bring trouble and suffering in the future, and to make the harder choices in the present that will nevertheless secure our lasting happiness.

Too many adults sacrifice the long-term happiness of a stable and united family, for the pleasure of a fleeting affair at the office. The law and the commandments of God are designed to teach us these lessons, not to spoil our fun, but to ensure our lasting felicity.

If we have learnt any of this wisdom as grandparents, we have a duty and a responsibility to pass it on to our children and our grandchildren. As the years of our own lives are coming to an end there is nothing better that we can do with what we have accumulated than to invest it in our children and our children's children. That goes for our money, but even more for our wisdom, such as it is, and to the knowledge and understanding of the world that we have, sometimes painfully, gained.

It may not be welcomed or accepted at the time, but at least we have tried. That is better than simply sitting back and watching the next generation flounder in that sea of uncertainty and conflicting ideas which is all that the world offers them today.

As older people we may despair of the way in which the world is going (every generation does). We cannot change the world; that is the aspiration and the prerogative of the young. But we can invest ourselves and our experience into the lives of those closest to us, and pass on to them whatever good inheritance we may have received ourselves and that we have built up over our own lifetime.

In older, tribal, societies it was the elders who were recognized as the repositories and the channels of this ancestral wisdom. Of course, ancestral wisdom, the tradition of the elders, is not always right, and the young must take it and test it for themselves, and probably adapt it for an ever-changing world. But the older generation is failing in its duty if it does not pass on its knowledge of how to live the good life to those who have yet to begin it.

Apart from anything that we can offer to our grandchildren, however, being a grandparent is one of the great rewards of old age. It enables us to enjoy all that is best about children without having to suffer all that is worst.

People often say that the best thing about grandchildren is that you can give them back at the end of the day. That is not the best: the best is the joy of listening to their chatter, enjoying their achievements step by step as they grow up, cuddling them and being cuddled by them, loving them and being loved by them, and all these joys without the toils and tribulations of being their parents. It is one of life's rare privileges: all gain and no pain.

Chapter Five

WHERE ARE YOU GOING TO LIVE?

During our working lives, the places where we have lived have probably been linked to the places where we have worked. This link will certainly become closer in the future as the cost of travel becomes higher and higher. Long commutes between home and work will become increasingly unaffordable.

But once we are free of work, we are free to live wherever we like - anywhere in the world. It is often the first question that people ask themselves about their retirement; where are we going to live? The freedom can be intoxicating.

Too often, however, the link that we have already noticed between the idea of retirement and the idea of holidays leads people to assume that the place in which they have enjoyed idyllic holidays will also provide the place for an idyllic retirement. It is rarely the case.

The best is yet to be

Somewhere that seemed like Paradise in the height of summer may be very dreary in the cold and rain of winter. We may have loved a fortnight of golf as a change from the desk or the classroom. But fifty-two weeks of golf may pall. Holiday resorts may be full of entertainment and alive with people during the season, but out of season they can turn into ghost towns.

Holidays are great, but as we have already seen, retirement is not the same thing as a holiday, and the best places for a holiday are not necessarily the best places for retirement. Neither Bournemouth nor Tenerife may be so inviting for the rest of your life as they were for a week's package tour.

This is particularly true of retirement abroad. For thirty or forty years the British have been lured to the Dordogne and the Costa del Sol by the availability of ruined French farmhouses and sun-drenched villas, all for a fraction of the cost of a house in crowded old England.

Books like Peter Mayle's *A Year in Provence* and endless television programmes about buying property abroad have encouraged others to live the dream. But, even after negotiating the labyrinths of French or Spanish law and bureaucracy, and even after negotiating with local builders with strong regional accents, there are still snags to be faced.

So used are we to living in our own countries, that it is not always apparent how different or how difficult it is to live in a foreign one.

We do indeed share a great deal of history and culture with our European neighbours, but there is also a great deal that we do not share with them, of which the language is only the most obvious.

Then again, we can be misled, by sharing a common language with the United States or Australia, into thinking that these countries are the same as home in Britain, only with more space. That is not true either. The United States, and even Australia, are in many ways more of a foreign country that France or Spain.

Moving house at any time is one of the most traumatic experiences that we undergo. Moving house and living in a foreign country is several times more stressful. Do we really need that kind of stress at our time of life?

The best is yet to be

Caroline and Richard decided that Richard's retirement was an opportunity to begin something new and adventurous together instead of just drifting into old age. They had had some great holidays together in France, so they decided that they would retire there.

At first there were seemingly endless dinner parties and ex-pat gatherings to attend. They also wanted to tour as much of France and Spain as possible. After one false start in the property market, they found a lovely, old, stone house, overlooking the Dordogne valley and five of its castles. Each spring they could open the doors and windows, and enjoy the beauty of the countryside and the wonderful summer weather, far into October. But there was a down-side to the idyll, which became increasingly apparent.

For Caroline and Richard, a major problem was the lack of the sort of lively church to which they had been accustomed. They missed the worship and the fellowship of other Christians, and found it difficult to find anyone to talk to, either in French or in English, about their faith.

As a result their friends and acquaintances did not have any idea of who they really were or of what really mattered to them. The shallowness of ex-patriot life soon became apparent, and it was difficult to make any real friendships with French people.

Language remained a problem. Caroline took lessons and became reasonably proficient, but still found it difficult to negotiate the labyrinths of French bureaucracy. The attitude of the local people was at best ambiguous, valuing the ex-patriots contribution to their local economy, but resenting their apparent wealth and their inevitable foreignness.

In Britain, we are only too familiar with our own resentments towards immigrants not to understand the same resentments in the local French or Spanish populations. Richard found the language harder to learn. He suffered a stroke, and although the French health service took excellent care of him, it left his memory impaired.

The weather itself also proved less idyllic as time went on. Summers sometimes became excessively hot with temperatures in the 40°s, and winters were wet and cold and the houses badly insulated and expensive to heat. Theatres and concerts were many kilometres away and as the cost of fuel increased, the sheer distances that had to be covered in France became an increasing problem.

When the exchange rate between the pound and the euro turned decisively against them, devaluing their pensions, Caroline and Richard turned for home. They came back to England, appreciating their own country, with all its difficulties, much more than when they went away. They had tried to integrate, to be polite and grateful, but, with a few exceptions, had felt themselves to be rebuffed and excluded by their French neighbours.

Jill and Malcolm had a different and happier experience. They retired to Spain for the benefit of Malcolm's health where the warm climate was better for his fibro-myalgia. Unlike Caroline and Richard, they found a sympathetic English-speaking church where they quickly became involved, leading a home group, pastorally supporting church members, and reaching out to befriend those on the fringe.

They discovered other ex-pat groups that went walking, organised art classes, showed films, and shared meals and parties together. The small town in which they lived provided a stimulating, multi-national community, with numerous opportunities for social life and making new friends. They continue to appreciate and enjoy the weather, the out-door life-style, fresh vegetables and fruit all the year round, the wine and the Mediterranean diet. But even for Jill and Malcolm there is a down-side.

Their family, children and grandchildren, all live in the English Midlands, and although the existence of cheap flights makes visiting possible, and the existence of e-mail and Skype makes contact easy, they are still a thousand miles apart.

Many of their friends, in the church and in the community, are people who live in England and only come to Spain for holidays and short visits. Language remains a problem for Jill and Malcolm too. Understanding the culture and the nuances of a country and its ways requires more than the linguistic ability to shop or order a meal in Spanish.

To English ex-pats the Spanish seem to tolerate a culture of bribery and corruption that would be unacceptable in Britain. There seems to be one set of laws for foreigners and another for the Spanish. As they grow older, Malcolm and Jill concede that they may eventually move back to Britain, but in the meanwhile they do not regret their move to Spain, in spite of the difficulties.

Nowhere is Paradise on earth. We lost Paradise on earth a long time ago, and we are not going to regain it here. One day when we die, by God's grace, we shall go to be in Paradise with Jesus, but not before.

Here and now, everywhere we live is a compromise between what we want and what we can get. The fact that these two couples have found that there are disadvantages as well as advantages to living abroad in retirement should not surprise us. But it should make us wary of imagining that moving abroad is the answer to all our troubles and the gateway to a new and carefree life.

The experience of these two couples should also help us to identify the real questions that we ought to ask about where we are going to live.

Where are you going to live?

As we consider the question of where we are going to live, we need to begin with the questions that we have already asked: what are we going to do all day? And, where are our family and friends? As we have seen with Caroline and Richard, and with Malcolm and Jill, for Christians at least, another vital question is, where are we going to worship?

Distances will become increasingly important factors in our lives as we grow older. Mobility decreases with age. We may not be able to walk as far or as fast as we used to do. There may come a time when we are not able to drive a car. Living down an unmade track, that quickly fills up with snow in winter, in a house that is three miles from the nearest shop, and twenty miles from the nearest hospital, is probably not a sensible choice for retirement. It may be an idyllic spot, peaceful and far removed from the hustle and bustle that we have endured for the past forty years, but the practical problems will become increasingly apparent.

These problems may affect others as well as ourselves. As we consider afresh our relationship with our families, distance is going to be an important factor in how those relationships work out, not only from the point of view of our seeing and helping them, but from the point of view of them seeing and helping us.

It is one of the duties and privileges of children to care for their aged parents, as their parents cared for them in their childhood. Honouring your father and your mother, as the Ten Commandments require us to do, is not only a matter of obedience when we are young, but of reciprocating our parents' love and care when they are old.

As retired people, we may find ourselves on both sides of this responsibility. More and more, retired people still have their own parents alive, and living into their late 80s and 90s. Many of the books about retirement examine the issues of caring for elderly parents, and the choices that have to be made for them.

Can we have them to live with us? At what point do we have to accept that they need the sort of nursing care that only a Residential or Nursing Home can give? How do we manage their financial affairs, perhaps by Power of Attorney, to ensure them the best comfort and attention that we and they can afford?

We may well find ourselves involved in these matters as we enter retirement, and retirement may give us an opportunity to devote more time and effort to repaying our aged parents. But we would be naïve if we did not recognise that sooner or later the boot is likely to be on the other foot, and that we are going to be the ones who need the love and care of our children.

Either way, we need to make these considerations important, if not the main ones, in choosing where we are going to live. To live near to aged parents and at the same time to live near children and grandchildren may not be possible; different phases of our life in retirement may mean moving more than once, but these are primary factors in planning the latter years of our lives.

Our own children began their married lives abroad. After about ten years, however, our daughter and her husband decided to return to England. There were several factors influencing their direction, but one significant one was that they were aware that both sets of grandparents were getting older and that sooner or later they would not want to find themselves nine thousand miles away from parents who were sick, infirm or dying. For the same reason, once they were settled back in England, my wife and I decided to move nearer to them in this country while we were still able to make the transition.

In the New Testament, the church takes responsibility for looking after and providing for widows and orphans (Acts 6:1). This was part of the general willingness of the early Christians to share their goods and possessions as any of them had need (Acts 4:34-35). We mostly learn about these arrangements from the Bible at times when things had gone wrong, but it remained a feature of life together in the church for several centuries. The church functioned as a surrogate family, taking its name and its character from God the Father (Ephesians 3:14).

At its best, the church still functions in this way towards its older members. But the Bible makes it clear that the primary responsibility for aged relatives lies with the natural family (1 Timothy 5:3-8). It appears from this passage in the first letter to Timothy that some families were leaving the care and provision of their elderly parents to the church, when they were capable of looking after them themselves. We see in our own society how easily State welfare provision can become a substitute for personal, family care.

If the Church or the State will take care of our old people for us, why, we think, do we need to bother? Neither the Church nor the State should acquiesce in this dereliction of our duty, and, thank God, many children do want to do the right thing and look after their aged parents as much as they can. We do not make it any easier for them if we choose to live many miles away.

Jesus said, 'A man's life does not consist of the abundance of his possessions' Luke 12:15). So of what does it consist? It consists in our relationships, first with God, then with other people. The decision about where we are going to live in retirement should look first at the matter of our relationships and how easy or difficult it will be to maintain them. We have just considered this in relation to our families, but it is not healthy either for us or our families if our lives are focussed exclusively on them. We also need friends.

We may have people with whom we have been friends all our lives or over a long period of time. Where do they live? They may of course, like our families, live all over the world or all over the country. But it may be that there is a particular region where they are concentrated.

Retirement may be an opportunity to see more of our friends. There are not usually many people whom we meet in the course of our lives with whom we form close and enduring friendships.

It is a matter of background, interests, temperament, shared experiences and some intangible factor that we might call sympathy. The French call it *sympathie*: it means, feeling drawn to someone. It is a rare phenomenon amongst all the people we meet, and therefore to be highly valued. It survives separation; when we meet again, it is as if the years have rolled away and we take up where we left off. Retirement is an opportunity to indulge such relationships and give them more time.

Retirement is also an opportunity to form new friendships. That will probably be linked to the things that we decide to do in our retirement. Friendships often come out of working together

94

or the interests that we share. Hobbies or leisure activities are not only to be valued for themselves and the interest or benefit that we obtain from them, but also as opportunities to meet new people and make new friends. Through the art class, the bridge club, or the ramblers association we are likely to find companions as much as past-times, and the one may be as important as the other.

For Christians, not the least important of all these relationships will be those with people who share our faith, and with whom we worship and work together in the Kingdom of God. The local church should be the family of believers in our one heavenly Father: spiritual brothers and sisters in the Lord Jesus. Therefore, as we try to balance up the attractions of different places for our retirement, we should not overlook the importance of finding a good, sympathetic church.

Anglicans are often obsessed with parish boundaries and feel an obligation to worship at the parish church. While in some places this may be the door into a whole new world of living faith, in other places it can be spiritually a living death. We live in the age of the motor car and public transport, and the walk or the ride to church is no more or less of an obstacle than that to any of the other facilities that we use each week.

The quality of the spiritual life and of the relationships in the church that we choose are more important than parish boundaries or denominations. But it is remarkable how many Christians moving to a new area in retirement research all the amenities that a town or village has to offer, but do not think about the question of church until the first Sunday after the removal van has pulled away.

When all the factors involving these many relationships have been weighed - our relationships with family and friends, our relationship to God - it is time to think about the sort of house or property that we need. The property web-sites offer the choice of houses, apartments/flats, bungalows and retirement properties.

Perhaps the first question is about gardens. Do you want a garden? If so, then of course you want a house or a bungalow. A block of flats or a retirement property might offer communal gardens and a place to sit outside, but not the sort of private garden in which you can grow your own plants or mow your own grass. Some people love gardening and make it almost a full-time occupation in retirement; others prefer to leave the weeding and mowing to others. Chacun à son gout.

As well as relieving you of the responsibilities of gardening, an apartment or a retirement property will also relieve you, in return for a considerable maintenance charge, of the responsibilities of maintaining your property. External decoration, window cleaning, fixing the leaks in the roof, and all the other unpredictable hazards of owning a house, are someone else's headache. It is worth thinking about this in the context of getting older, less able or inclined to climb ladders and Do-It-Yourself.

Then, there is the question of the area and the surroundings. A central location may be ideal for shopping and buses, but there may also be fumes from the traffic by day and noisy revellers at night. On the other hand, peace and quiet may come at the price of a bus ride or a walk into town.

Finally, what you want and what you can afford may be two different things. It is not worth having a dream house and garden if every day is dominated by worries about how to make ends meet. Too much capital tied up in the house, and you have too little left to replace the car or fund the grandchildren through university. Too much income swallowed up in Council Tax, insurance, and utility bills, leaves too little for treats for you or yours, and maybe too little for everyday housekeeping and hair-cuts.

Make up your mind, if you have not done so before this time in your lives, that everything involves a trade-off. It is almost inconceivable that one house or flat is going to satisfy all the criteria that you have drawn up for your ideal retirement.

In the end, the decision about where we are going to live in retirement may be to stay put. A few people, though an ever-decreasing proportion of the population, spend all their lives in the same place, even in the same house. Only a few years ago I conducted the funeral of an old man who had died in the same cottage in which he had been born. He had grown up there during the First World War; he had never married or moved away but had stayed at home and looked after his parents there until they died; then he had lived there on his own even after his retirement from the farm on which he had worked all his life, and finally expired in the same bedroom in which he had slept for nearly ninety years.

Even without such a degree of stability as that, many people have put down roots in a place over many years, and by the time they retire it is too late to pull them up and start again somewhere new.

As a Church of England vicar, my wife and I spent our lives living in parsonage houses, tied to the job. Having accepted the job, it was a matter of, 'This is the house: live in it.' And we did. It involved living in everything from a flat upstairs in a converted terrace house in Lancashire, with a front door beside the school dustbins and the smell of boiled cabbage from the school kitchen, to a medieval manor house with an acre and a half of land, including a paddock and a pond, a kitchen garden and a circular gravel drive.

We made the best of it. Most people, most of the time, have more choice in the matter, but the principle is worth learning: make the best of it, whatever 'it' may be. It may not be ideal, but any house in this world is only a tent.

We pitch our tent somewhere for the time being, but we are not here to stay. This world is not our home. We are strangers here, only passing through. It is a mistake, either to become too attached to a place, or to make too much of a fuss about its drawbacks. One day we shall have to move on in any case. Our eternal home is in heaven, and that will be the best home we have ever had.

Meanwhile, perhaps the best question to ask about retirement housing is, where can we make ourselves most easily available, to our families, to our friends, to those whom we might be able to serve in retirement.

Chapter Six

PAST AND PRESENT

There is a poem of Laurence Binyon that speaks of the autumn of life. It is called *The Burning of the Leaves*:

Now is the time for the burning of the leaves.
They go to the fire; the nostril pricks with smoke
Wandering slowly into a weeping mist.
Brittle and blotched, ragged and rotten sheaves!
A flame seizes the smouldering ruin and bites
On stubborn stalks that crackle as they resist.

The last hollyhock's fallen tower is dust;
All the spices of June are a bitter reek,
All the extravagant riches spent and mean.
All burns! The reddest rose is a ghost;
Sparks whirl up, to expire in the mist: the wild
Fingers of fire are making corruption clean.

The best is yet to be

Now is the time for stripping the spirit bare,
Time for the burning of days ended and done,
Idle solace of things that have gone before:
Rootless hope and fruitless desire are there;
Let them go to the fire, with never a look behind.
The world that was ours is a world that is ours no
more.

They will come again, the leaf and the flower, to arise
From squalor of rottenness into the old splendour,
And magical scents to a wondering memory bring;
The same glory, to shine upon different eyes.
Earth cares for her own ruins, naught for ours.
Nothing is certain, only the certain spring.

For me, the poem conjures up memories of autumn bonfires slowly burning through the stalks and leaves from flower-beds and shrubberies in vast vicarage gardens. It speaks of looking forward to the 'certain spring', but it also speaks of the need to deal with the remnants of the past, with memories, of both glory and pain, of both the 'extravagant riches' of the past as well as its 'rootless hopes and fruitless desires.'

102

Past and present

Older people are supposed to spend a lot of their time thinking about the past, and some of them do. It is better still to spend time thinking about the glory that is to be revealed, but we do need to think about the past and to sort out our thoughts about it and, maybe, to sort out some of our past mistakes and put our houses in order before it is too late.

We all have good memories: of the people who have loved and cared for us, of successes and achievements, of exams passed and matches won, of letters that have brought good news and of long-awaited reunions.

There have been times in our lives when we have been happy: summer holidays, evenings by the fire, the day she said 'Yes', the birth of the first child. These are good things to remember, but even here there is a danger: nostalgia, the 'idle solace of things that have gone before'. Nostalgia is regret: regret that those days are over and will never come again and, unless we are careful, this regret will turn into bitterness with regard to the present, and none of this is healthy or helpful. Beware of nostalgia, and do not indulge in it.

The healthy way to remember the good things of the past is with thankfulness. I knew a wonderful old lady who lived to be nearly one hundred. For the last decade of her life she was frail and suffered from great difficulty in swallowing. But she was unfailingly cheerful and kept repeating, 'I have had a wonderful life.'

Her face would light up as she thanked God for all his goodness to her, for her parents, her husband and her children, her grandchildren and great-grandchildren, the wonderful ways in which God had revealed himself to her and the hope she had of going to be with him.

She would clasp her hands together in delight as she recounted her blessings and told them one by one. As a consequence she never wanted for visitors, who departed with their own spirits lifted and with a renewed thankfulness for the blessings of their own lives.

There is an old Christian hymn that may seem corny to some people but which contains some very wise advice:

Past and present

Count your blessings, name them one by one,
Count your blessings, see what God hath done.
Count your blessings, name them one by one,
And it will surprise you what the Lord hath done.

The church's liturgy reminds us that 'at all times and in all places it is our duty and our joy to give God thanks and praise'. Our memories of good times past are always with us and are an incentive to be thankful.

But not all our memories are good ones. We all have regrets. Some of our regrets are coupled with a sense of guilt and shame at the things that we have done. Others are coupled with a sense of disappointment, of failure or rejection. These things come back particularly to haunt us in the middle of the night; they may trouble us less during the daytime, but how do we deal with them? We should not sweep them under the carpet as we draw back the curtains in the morning, but bring them into the light and examine them.

First, there is our sense of guilt. For every one of us from an early age there are things that we have done that we wish we had not done, and for which we realize that we deserve some sort of punishment.

In childhood it is the threat of parents or teachers finding out what we have done that fills us with dread: we know that there will be a price to pay. As adults we have the same dread of our misdoings coming to light. There might not be the same threat of punishment, unless we have committed a crime in the eyes of the law, but we know that there would be a sense of shame if people knew the truth about us, and we shrink from it.

We are ashamed in our own eyes, even if not in the eyes of others, and then there are the eyes of God. We may escape exposure to the prying eyes of the world, but there is another One, 'to whom all hearts are open, all desires known, and from whom no secrets are hidden.' How will we face him when the time comes? Is there anywhere that forgiveness is to be found for our sins and shortcomings?

Kingsley Amis was a successful and well-known 20th century novelist. He was also by his own admission a serial adulterer. He and his wife Hilary were divorced in 1965, after seventeen years of marriage, because of his affairs with other women. Both married again. Yet Amis seems to have retained a love for Hilary and she for him, for in his old age his sons arranged for him to be cared for in the home of Hilary and her third husband Alastair Boyd.

Amis was also a notorious drinker. In his younger days his prodigious drinking was social, but according to Clive James, Amis reached a turning point when his drinking ceased to be social, and became a way of dulling his remorse and regret at his behaviour towards Hilly.

"Amis had turned against himself deliberately... it seems fair to guess that the troubled grandee came to disapprove of his own conduct."

In an interview in The Times before his death, Amis confessed, 'I carry my sins around with me daily. I have no one to forgive me.'

I hope that no one who reads this book, will come to the end and be able to say, 'I have no one to forgive me.' For we all have someone to forgive us, if we will only accept him as our Lord and Saviour. He is Jesus. He died on the cross that we might be forgiven. He is the Lamb of

God who takes away the sin of the world, your sins and mine, and Kingsley Amis's, had he but known it and received it.

There is no sin so great, so shameful, that Jesus cannot and will not say to us, 'Bring it to me. Give it to me. I have borne worse than that.' He was called Jesus from his birth because he came to save his people from their sins. The name Jesus means 'The Lord saves.'

There is no other Saviour. A friend can forgive me the wrong that I did to him, but he cannot forgive me the wrongs that I have done to others. Only God can forgive sins, as even the Pharisees knew. God took flesh and dwelt among us. He was born in Bethlehem: Immanuel, God with us. He lived among us, walked among us, spoke to us, did many mighty works among us, died for our sins and rose again from the dead.

Abraham and Moses did not die for my sins. Mohammed did not die for my sins. The Buddha did not die for my sins. There is only one sacrifice, full, perfect, and sufficient, for the sins of the world, and that is the sacrifice of himself that Jesus made upon the Cross. But it is sufficient.

Past and present

We can bring all our memories of guilt and shame to the foot of the cross, and there find forgiveness and peace. If we have never done so before, it is a liberating experience to go systematically through our memories of the past, and write down a list of all the things that trouble us, the things that we have done wrong of which our conscience is afraid, and confess them to God one by one.

In my own experience it is even more liberating to do this in the presence of some discreet pastor or priest, who can assure us of Gods' forgiveness. There is nothing as liberating as revealing the very worst about ourselves, not only to God but also to a fellow human being, who will respect our confidence, but who will also assure us of the infinite compassion and mercy of Almighty God.

I have loved to hear the words of the absolution spoken over me:

'Our Lord Jesus Christ has left power to his church to absolve all sinners who truly repent, and by his authority committed unto me, I absolve you from all your offenses, in the name of the Father, the Son and the Holy Spirit.'

There is nothing more important than putting ourselves right with God at any time of our lives but not least in retirement; to put ourselves right by repentance, confession, and receiving reconciliation with God through the Blood of Jesus.

But then we also need to do whatever we can to put right our relationships with the other people whose lives we have damaged through our wrong-doing. With some there may no longer be any chance of doing this because they themselves have already died. All we can do then is to ask God to convey to them, wherever they may be, our sorrow and regret at the wrong that we did to them, and our forgiveness of them for the wrong that they may have done to us. But alive or dead, we need to do our best to be reconciled with those our lives have touched to our mutual hurt.

To those we have hurt by our words and deeds we need to apologise, to say sorry and, if there are any practical steps that we can take, to make amends if only by a gesture. There is no guarantee that such an approach will be welcomed or accepted, but the Apostle Paul only requires us 'to live at peace with everyone, *as far as it depends on you*' (Romans 12:18). We are not responsible for how our overtures towards reconciliation are received.

By the same token our forgiveness of those who have sinned against us does not depend on their repentance. Forgiveness is first and foremost a refusal to hold a grudge or to seek revenge. Rather it is a resolution to do good to those who have hurt us in any way that we can.

It is the will that counts, rather than our practical ability to put our good desires into effect. The least, and perhaps the best, that we can do for them is to pray for them, for their salvation and for their reconciliation.

All this may involve letters or phone calls as well as prayers, a Christmas or a birthday card, a bunch of flowers or a drink in a bar: words and gestures that offer a renewal of friendship before it is too late.

One of the best uses to which we can put some of our free time in retirement is in restoring friendships and relationships that have turned sour or gone wrong in years gone by. Those relationships may never blossom again as they once did, but we, and, we hope, those to whom we speak, will find peace and freedom from at least one source of regret.

But perhaps a harder form of regret to deal with is regret, not over the things that we have done, but over the things that life has done to us - our disappointments. So many of us have suffered disappointment, through no obvious fault of our own or of other people, but just through the way life has turned out: disappointments in love, someone else getting the girl or the boy that we wanted or never meeting the right person at all; the disappointment of childlessness; of failing a crucial exam at school; of being rejected after an interview; of being passed over for promotion.

Life is not fair in any obvious sense of the word, and we are often tempted to compare our lot with that of others, their parents, their home, their school, their job, their partner, their children, their wealth, their holidays, their life-style.

It is called envy or covetousness, and it is corrosive of our peace of mind, even if it does not lead us into worse sins. But envy is the other side of the coin of disappointment.

We are disappointed with our own lot and envious of the lot of others. Thankfulness is at least a partial remedy for all this, as it is for some of the other diseases of the soul that we have examined before. But there is a fact that is not often remarked upon: that the remedy for our guilt, that we have also examined before, is also a remedy for our disappointments. We can take our disappointments as well as our sins to the foot of the Cross and find there solace for our grief.

In the Protestant tradition of Christianity we overlook the fact that for a thousand years the ideal Christian life was thought to be one of poverty, chastity and obedience, the life of the monk or nun, enclosed in a community of worship and prayer. Rightly or wrongly, Protestants rejected this ideal as a withdrawal from the world that Christ came to redeem, and it is certainly true that the consequence of this idealization of the life of renunciation has been that the Catholic tradition has offered little in the way of guidance or example to the Christian men and women who have continued to live 'in the world,' a life of sex and marriage, of families and children, of business and industry, of making money and paying the bills.

But the strength of the monastic ideal was that it mirrored the earthly life of Jesus. Jesus was poor, chaste and obedient to his heavenly Father. He was detached from possessions; he had nowhere to lay his head. When he died, all the property he had was the clothes he stood up in. Jesus had no love affairs, no wife, no children. From childhood, he had no ambition except to be about his Father's business, to be obedient to God throughout his life. This obedience led to his death in his early thirties, a life cut short in its prime.

This life, this death, this Jesus, is the place and the person to which to bring our disappointments, in order to see them in a new perspective and a new light. The only real failure in life is our failure to live our lives in obedience to God, to be about his business for us, whatever that business might be.

God's business does not have to be something overtly religious. Eric Liddell, whose story is told in the film *Chariots of Fire,* was called to be about his Father's business as a missionary in

China, but first the Father's business for Eric was to be a runner and to compete in the Olympic Games in 1924. His dedication to his running was a problem for some of his more dour Scots brethren, but Liddell was as clear that running was a vocation as much as a call to China.

So for us, being about our Father's business may mean marriage and family as much as celibacy; working as an electrician or a farmer, as much as being a missionary; making money in industry or commerce as much as renouncing property as a monk. The only real success is faithfulness to whatever God calls us to do.

Happy the person who sets out, like Jesus, from the age of twelve to be obedient to God, to seek and to do his will. That person need never be afraid of disappointment. Unlike Jesus, we shall fail to be obedient in things great and small, but our reward still lies in renewing our obedience in whatever new circumstances we find ourselves.

There is another old song, that again may seem corny to some, but that also points us to a profound spiritual truth, a truth that dissolves the pain of disappointed hopes and renews our love for the one who has saved us, not only from our sins but also from our disappointments:

> *Turn your eyes upon Jesus,*
> *Look full on his wonderful face,*
> *And the things of the world will grow*
> *strangely dim,*
> *In the light of his glory and grace.*

The last sort of negative memories with which we have to deal are those which have damaged our sense of self-worth, the memories of events that left us with a sense of rejection. These memories can become increasingly difficult when we retire because for many of us our sense of self-worth has been built upon the work that have done.

'What do you do?' is one of the first questions that we ask of a new acquaintance. Our identity is closely bound up with the jobs that we do. 'I am a teacher, or a mother, an engineer, or a deep-sea diver,' we reply, as the case may be.

So who are we when we cease to be any of these things? Now, the answer seems to be, 'I am nothing,' and that is difficult.

Establishing a sense of our identity, of who we are and of what we are worth, is one of the first works of childhood, and it continues throughout our lives. The first and most important sense of my identity that I need, even from the womb, is that I am someone lovable and beloved.

In establishing this sense of identity there is no substitute for loving parents, people who have loved and treasured us from the moment of conception onwards, and who have gone on loving and cherishing us through all the changes and chances of childhood and growing up. With loving parents, a foundation of self-esteem and self-assurance is laid in us that will never be entirely destroyed whatever else may happen to us. But of course for many people that foundation in infancy and childhood was lacking, and for all of us it was incomplete.

There are no perfect parents, which is why we all need to know God, the perfect Father in heaven: the perfect father, the perfect parent that we never had.

Some people say that they cannot relate to God as Father because their own experience of being fathered was so bad. But that is to miss the point. We all need to come to know God as the Father that, consciously or unconsciously, we all longed to have, but never actually had. And we only come to know God as Father through Jesus.

It is only through coming to know the love of God, the enduring, never-failing, unchanging, monotonous, affirming love of God for us, that we finally discover who we are and what we are worth. We are his children, created for his glory, redeemed by his blood, welcomed, accepted, loved, forever and ever.

People may have rejected us at various points in our lives, from conception onwards, at home, at school, at work, our families, our friends, our colleagues. We may have been despised, mocked, ostracized, made to feel worthless, but God never treated us so.

He has hated what has been done to us as much as we did. Even now he wants to reassure us, to build us up in our own eyes by seeing ourselves, not as others have seen us, but as he has seen us, as a beloved man, woman or child. His love does not depend on what we have done, either good or bad.

We can never earn his love, nor forfeit his love. Like all true love it is freely given, and asks nothing of us, except to be loved in return. And how can we not return such love?

All the things at which we have looked in this chapter we should have known and practiced all our lives. But many of us come to the years of retirement without knowing any of them, or with a backlog of unhealed relationships and unresolved emotions.

Part of the business of retirement is to clear out the attics of the mind, to buff up the good memories and put them on display in our trophy cabinets for the enjoyment of at least our own thankful eyes. It is also to dispose of the junk memories, to bring into the light the incriminating ones, to account for them properly to God and to others, to mend the things that have been broken, to sort out the memories that trouble us and lay them to rest so that we can sleep peacefully at night for the rest of our days.

Chapter Seven

'GOD SEE ME THROUGH'

Life falls into three parts. The first thirty years of life (give or take a few years) is a time of beginnings. Our lives are full of new things. We learn new things first at home then at school, from saying our first words, to the mysteries of quantum mechanics; we acquire new skills, from feeding ourselves, to playing Mozart piano concertos; we achieve new degrees of independence, from cycling to school on our own, to taking a gap year in Australia; we discover new pleasures, from the pleasures of wine, to the pleasures and heartaches of love.

Children and young people are always looking forward, eager for the next stage of life, from infancy to childhood, from childhood to adolescence, from adolescence to adulthood. The next birthday is always being anticipated: 'When I am five … sixteen … twenty-one ...'

Each year is another step up the ladder, opening up fresh horizons and disclosing new opportunities. It is not always a happy time of life, not all childhood experiences are good ones, and some people's experiences of childhood are appalling.

As with every time of life, there are challenges and difficulties to be faced and overcome that are peculiar to that stage of development, but in principle, youth is a time of exciting new prospects and hopes.

The second stage of life is the years of maturity, let us say, from the age of thirty to sixty (give or take a few years). It is during these years that we can make a difference to the world, at least to the world around us, that we can use the gifts and opportunities that we have been given to achieve our goals and fulfil whatever purposes we may have conceived for ourselves or for others.

By the age of thirty, we have usually completed formal education and acquired some useful skills; by then we should have chosen and embarked upon some sort of career, even if that career may be subject to further development or

121

change; we should be married and ready to start a family, unless God has called us to celibacy; we should have worked out the answers to the questions of our faith and values.

These middle years of our lives are the time of our greatest potential for fruitfulness. Our physical strength and health are at their peak: it is the time for action and achievement, for finding satisfaction in our work and a sense of accomplishment.

As in the first phase of life, there are challenges and difficulties that are peculiar to these years, and our lives do not always work out as we had hoped or as we would have wished. We have already looked at the issue of dealing with disappointments and regrets. But these are the years that are given to us to achieve something, for God, for others, for our families, for ourselves.

The third and final stage of life is old-age, the stage at which we have arrived when we retire from full-time paid employment. This is a time in our lives when what is happening to us is the opposite of what happened in our childhood.

Our strength and our abilities are decreasing as the years go by. Our horizons are narrowing rather than widening. We are forgetting more rather than learning more, or at least forgetting more than we learn. The greater part of our lives is now behind us rather than in front of us. We tend to be backward looking, rather than forward looking.

This is the greatest challenge of old age. How do we avoid the trap of feeling sorry for ourselves and envying the young their vigour and their youth? It is not easy to watch children and young people doing all the things we used to do, and no longer be able to do them ourselves. It is not easy to see young men and women with the bloom of youth on their skin, to see their optimism and vitality, and not compare them with ourselves, with our wrinkles and our aches and pains. Old age is inevitably a time of diminution.

From the age of fourteen I enjoyed the pleasure of holidays spent sailing on the Norfolk Broads. These were days each year spent in a world apart, no houses, no roads, no engines, no telephones, completely dependent on the wind and the weather. It was at once a relaxation, and a challenge of an entirely different sort.

After we were married my wife and I continued to spend a week on the Broads each year; then we took our children, and then continued to go on our own again after the children were grown up. Then, one year on the Broads, when I was approaching sixty, I suddenly felt, 'I cannot be bothered any longer with all the heaving and hauling, the struggling with wet canvas and the quant pole. It is time to stop.'

One by one, for many different reasons as we grow older, we have to let go of pleasures and activities that were once important and pleasurable to us. Growing old gracefully is easier said than done.

Many older people seem to avoid the presence and the company of the young. Some complain vociferously if the neighbours' children are noisy or boisterous, as if children were ever anything else.

Old people's housing complexes seem to be popular, not only because they relieve the aged of some of the responsibilities of home ownership and provide the reassurance of a warden or manager, but also because they offer a child and youth free environment, in which we are less forcefully reminded of the vitality and pleasures we once enjoyed but now have lost.

Catherine Fox once suggested in a newspaper article, that old men were grumpy because they could no longer pounce on attractive young women like they used to do (and old women were grumpy because they were no longer the attractive young women who were pounced upon). Catherine Fox had a point. How do we avoid the grumpiness of old age that comes from a sense that we are excluded from so many of the activities in which younger people engage and which the world at large regards as the essence of life?

Part of the answer is to focus our minds on the blessings that we now enjoy rather than on the blessings that we once enjoyed. In the days of our sailing on the Norfolk Broads, it was even then a pleasure to come home afterwards: to sleep in a proper bed instead of a narrow bunk; if the weather had been wet, to get properly dry instead of living in clammy clothes all day; to cook on a proper stove instead of crouching over a gas-ring on the floor.

Old age is a time for enjoying the comforts of hearth and home, of strolling rather than rushing about, of reading and listening, of sitting still and watching the sun set or the leaves fall.

On one occasion in my youth, some friends and I spent a week sailing on the English Channel. We set out one day to cruise down towards Devon. We were caught in a gale that stirred the sea up into a most uncomfortable, if not dangerous, chop. We were as sick as dogs.

At dawn the following day we made for a harbour on the Isle of Wight to shelter until the gale blew over. I shall never forget the sense of relief as we entered the calm and safety of the breakwater, tied the yacht up and fell into beds that were no longer pitching and rolling about beneath us.

Old age should be a time of calm like that. We have navigated, more or less successfully, the storms of life and can now tie up alongside other boats that have survived the gale and entered the haven that they longed for.

As it says in the book Ecclesiastes, there is time for everything, and God has made everything beautiful in its time (Ecclesiastes 3:1, 11). The secret of contentment as our times change is to recognise those good things that are the particular blessings of each period in our lives and enjoy them while they last. One of the differences between youth and old age is that while the young think that they will never grow old, the old know that once they were young and that the young will grow old in time.

One of our services to the young is to give them an example of how to grow old without resentment by embracing the blessings of our own time of life and leaving them free to enjoy the blessings of theirs.

But not all the features of old age can be counted as blessings: old age has its sufferings with which we must also reckon. Not that old age is unique in this; every stage of life has its own trials and tribulations. As we see children playing together, we tend to forget that the school playground was a jungle, with its bullies and gangs, and its unwritten rules that had to be obeyed.

As we see the young falling in love and pairing up we tend to forget the misery of 'she loves me, she loves me not.' As we see young families out together, we tend to forget the sleepless nights with babies, the tantrums of the two-year-olds and the sulky teenagers. As we see people setting off to work in the mornings, we tend to forget the monotony of much of it, the anxiety of the forthcoming 'reorganisation', or the people climbing over each other's backs for promotion.

All that is behind us in old age, but we now have other struggles and sufferings of our own.

Life requires courage. Never mind taking part in the D-Day Landings or being the first man on the moon, just living an ordinary life requires courage. From the courage of the child learning to ride a bike, to the courage of the student leaving home to go to university, to the courage involved in getting married, we need courage to grow old and to die.

The prospects can be frightening: physical and mental decline, bereavement and loneliness, loss of control over our lives, and the final loss of control that we call death. Everyone needs courage to face these things.

Some of our sufferings or diminishments will be physical ones. Shakespeare characterised old age as 'sans teeth, sans eyes, sans taste, sans everything.' It is indeed a time when things tend to fall out, like hair and teeth; we tend to need aids, for hearing, for seeing, for walking. When my wife and I are asked by some health professional what medication we are taking, they seem surprised to hear that we are taking none. There seems to be an expectation that retired people will be on some regular dosage of drugs and pills. My wife and I are certainly blessed that we are not – yet.

Whatever aches and pains we may develop in old age, it is a mistake to think or talk too much about them. Our friends and relations do not want 'an organ recital' every time they come to see us. Our aches and pains are a bore, for us and for them. If our minds are still in good working order we need to keep them occupied with other concerns, more interesting than ourselves: world affairs, local affairs, church affairs, the things that we have seen and read, other people's doings and achievements, other people's sufferings.

Old age and its frailties should not turn us in upon ourselves, and if our mobility is reduced and our personal world becomes confined to our own neighbourhood or even our own four walls we can still look outward beyond them, watch, listen and pray.

Of all the sufferings that can afflict us in old age the worst are undoubtedly the spiritual ones at which we have already looked earlier in the book: disappointment and despair, guilt and remorse, bitterness and unforgiveness. Not only does such a soul experience acute anguish of its own, but its anguish also poisons and infects the body.

Many of the chronic physical diseases of old age are the result of accumulations of these unhealthy emotions over a lifetime. Happy is the person who has dealt with these attitudes as they have arisen and not let them fester. It may even be that all our physical diseases can ultimately be traced to our own bad habits, of body, mind or spirit.

The links, for example, between smoking and heart and lung disease, or between obesity and diabetes, are obvious and direct. But maybe there are other links that we do not so easily appreciate, for example between bitterness and arthritis, or anxiety and ulcers.

Who knows how much physical disease is in the last resort psychosomatic?

The world that God made was 'very good', which means that God did not create us to be ill. We are equipped with a very effective immune system that enables us to resist the effects of malignant organisms. Our bodies are also able to repair and renew themselves in amazing ways.

It is only when these mechanisms break down that we become ill and suffer. But none of us are sinless or perfect and we all share the inheritance of Adam, which is to die. All our diseases and infirmities are but a precursor or foretaste of death.

Not for nothing does a sick person say that they feel like death: they are indeed experiencing death nibbling away at their bodies. Each illness that we suffer is a little attack of death, which may be staved off for a season, but not forever.

As we grow older these little attacks of death become more frequent and more chronic. We can look to God to heal us and to save us, but we cannot escape the sentence of death that hangs over the whole human race, or its forerunner, the increasing frailties of old age.

A tranquil spirit enables us to bear physical suffering with relative equanimity. St Theresa of Avila, as a young woman, endured four years of intense physical suffering that took her to the very threshold of the grave, but during those years her communion with God was unbroken and she emerged from the ordeal not just spiritually unharmed, but strengthened.

People sometimes say that they are not afraid of death but are afraid of what they will have to go through before death. They have misplaced those fears. We ought to be very afraid of dying *without* God, but we need have no fear of suffering *with* God.

Perhaps the most distressing form of infirmity in old age is dementia. The body and the spirit can remain strong and intact but the mind slowly loses its grip on reality and its ability to process and retain information. The condition is distressing for the sufferer and for those who have to watch and care for the patient.

As with advancing physical decay, there comes a time when the resources for care in the home are exhausted. Thank God that there are then nursing homes and agencies that are available to fill the gaps, and, we hope, provide dignity and care until the end. Nothing in this world lasts forever. That can seem like a tragedy when we are well and happy, but when we are ill and suffering, it is a mercy. Even the worst and most humiliating sufferings of old age will end one day, and it is important as always to keep looking forward and not back.

In the life of the world to come there will no more death or mourning or crying or pain (Revelation 21:4), no more false teeth and Zimmer frames, no more Nursing Homes, not even any more spots (good news for the young) or wrinkles (good news for the old) (Ephesians 5:27).

Bill had been a fighter pilot during the Second World War. He was one of 'the few' praised by Winston Churchill in 1940 as the saviours of the nation during the Battle of Britain. After the War,

Bill married and pursued a successful career as a civil engineer. He and Pat retired to Norfolk, where they spent their old age peacefully surrounded by their cats and their garden.

Both had been born again as Christians in middle age and enjoyed the fellowship of a lively local church. As he approached eighty, Bill began to display the signs of Alzheimer's disease or senile dementia. Pat looked after him and nursed him at home for several years as he slowly declined.

Eventually he went to see the medical specialist who had been monitoring his condition. Pat was at the end of her own resources and Bill needed the sort of attention day and night that only a nursing home could give. The specialist asked Bill the usual series of questions, 'Which day of the week is it? Who is the Prime Minister?' To which questions Bill could give no answer.

Bill was invited to write down his own name, which he could not do either. He was asked to copy some shapes that the doctor had drawn on a piece of paper. That also was beyond him.

At last the doctor understood that Bill's links with the world around him had almost completely gone, and he turned away to discuss Bill's future care with Pat. But Bill reached out for the pencil and paper that the doctor had been using to test him. Without prompting, Bill then proceeded to write a coherent message of his own, 'God see me through.'

God did. Bill spent another two years in a nursing home, gradually deteriorating both mentally and physically. No one knows what goes on in the minds of those who suffer such dementia; they are unable to tell us. But God did see Bill through, and those are the words inscribed on his tombstone in the churchyard where he was finally buried: 'GOD SEE ME THROUGH.' It would be a good motto for all of us as we face the uncertainties of old age.

Of all the diminishments that we suffer in old age, perhaps the hardest to bear is bereavement. It is difficult to know whether it was Bill or Pat who suffered more through his long dementia. Alzheimer's disease has been called 'the long good-bye.' Long or short, old age is marked by good-byes to those whom we have loved. Our parents, brothers and sisters, friends, colleagues and contemporaries, we see many of them passing away before us.

There is a time in our lives when we always seem to be attending weddings, probably including our own, but also those of our friends and brothers and sisters. Then comes a period of attending baptisms or christenings, as we all produce children together. Last of all there comes a time of life when we are always going to funerals, including one day our own.

Of all the ways in which old age strips us down, this is perhaps the hardest to bear, the stripping away of the people whom we have loved and on whom we depended. When we marry we promise 'to love and to cherish till death do us part.' When we say those words to each other we are probably not thinking too much about that time when death will part us, but one day it comes.

However long an illness or infirmity our partner may have suffered, and however long we may have anticipated the moment of parting, nothing can prepare us for the awful pain of grief that seizes us in the pit of the stomach and seems as if it will never let go.

David lost his wife Sue after some forty years of marriage; a year later he was still writing, 'Life is miserable without her.' The activities of daily life resume for most of us and we carry on; the pain subsides, but the loss endures. We may pretend to others that we have got over it, but we cannot pretend to ourselves.

In the providence of God there must be a good purpose in this process of our gradually losing our physical and mental powers, our friends and our family. We must be able to say with Job, 'The Lord gave and the Lord has taken away. Blessed be the name of the Lord' (Job 1:28).

Like so many of the providences of God, his purposes may be clearer with hindsight, but part of the answer must be that, as we have noticed before, we need to shift the focus of our attention away from the things of this world to the things of the world to come.

The apostle Paul probably wrote the Second Letter to the Corinthians when he was in his middle fifties. He had spent some twenty years preaching the gospel, the last ten years in almost incessant journeys, planting new churches in Asia Minor and Greece. He had experienced numerous hardships and had often been close to death (2 Corinthians 11:23-27). With life expectancy then much lower than it is today, Paul must have recognized that death, whether at the hands of his opponents or from natural causes, must be nearer now than the time when he first believed.

With all this in mind, he wrote one of my favorite passages in the Bible; one that, to me, applies to the whole process of growing old and dying:

> *Therefore we do not lose heart. Though outwardly we are wasting away, yet inwardly we are being renewed day by day. For our light and momentary troubles are achieving for us an eternal glory that far outweighs them all. So we fix our eyes not on what is seen, but on what is unseen. For what is seen is temporary, but what is unseen is eternal.*

2 Corinthians 4:16-18

We do ourselves no favour in old age if we continue to fix our eyes on the things that are seen, because those things, whatever they are, will soon be taken away, and where will we be then?

There was an old woman who lived in extreme poverty in one of the townships of South Africa. Her daughter died of AIDS, leaving her to care for two small children. One by one these children died too, leaving the old woman, alone and destitute. Her testimony was: 'I never knew that Jesus was all I needed, until Jesus was all I had.'

The diminishments of old age are a challenge to our values. What are the things that we truly value, and in what order? In the end life is not about what happens or what we have in this world, but about what happens and what we will have in the world to come.

This life is a test-bed, a preparation, a training for the life of the world to come. I believe that the diminution of our earthly powers and activities is God's way of turning our minds away from the temporal and transient to the things that never pass away: God himself, his glory, his Son, his promises, his everlasting arms, the world to come and our eternal home.

It is impossible to overestimate the difference that it makes to us as we face the trials of old age if we can look beyond them to the life of the world to come. Paul again says, when thinking of the death of our loved ones in Christ, 'We do not grieve as others do who have no hope' (1 Thessalonians 4:13). But neither do we face old age for ourselves as others do who have no hope.

Those who believe in Jesus, in him who suffered, died and rose again, can look forward to rising again with him when their own sufferings are over. Death is not the end for those who are already alive in Christ. What lies before us is infinitely better than anything that lies behind.

Paul, in yet another letter, was thinking of the persecutions that he had suffered and was expecting to suffer, but his words can be applied to whatever suffering we may undergo as we approach the end ourselves: 'I consider that our present sufferings are not worth comparing with the glory that will be revealed to us' (Romans 8:18).

But, when all is said and done, there is no use pretending that it is easy growing old. A former mentor of mine, Charles Browne, used to say to me, 'Our technological age looks at everything as if it were a problem to be solved. But not all things are problems to be solved; some are burdens to be borne.'

There is a prayer of John Wesley that is used in the annual Methodist Covenant Service:

I am no longer my own but thine.
Put me to what thou wilt,
rank me with whom thou wilt.
Put me to doing, put me to suffering.
Let me employed for thee or laid aside for thee,
exalted for thee or brought low for thee.
Let me be full, let me be empty.
Let me have all things, let me have nothing.
I freely and heartily yield all things to thy pleasure and disposal.

This is an easy prayer to recite, but not an easy prayer to live, especially when we are confronted with the diminishments of old age. The 18th century French Jesuit, Jean Pierre de Caussade, spoke of 'the sacrament of the present moment.' In every moment, he said, God is giving us either a pleasure to enjoy, a duty to do, or a suffering to be borne.

We can find God in all three; enjoying the pleasures with thankfulness, doing our duties with diligence, bearing our sufferings with patience. God can only be met in the present moment. He cannot be met in the past; he cannot be met in the future; he can only be met in the present. But God is there to be met in the present moment, whatever the moment may hold.

Chapter Eight

MAKING A GOOD END

Our ancestors spoke of 'making a good end.' They realized that there is good way to die and a bad way to die. In the Litany in the 17th century Anglican Book of Common Prayer we pray to be delivered 'from battle and from murder and from sudden death.' It was thought important that we prepare ourselves for death, prepare to do the job properly, rather than be caught unawares.

It is rather a contrast to the prevailing sentiment today, which counts the person who collapses suddenly with a heart attack as the lucky one. But we create a lot of extra trouble for those we leave behind if we do not make reasonable preparations for our departure – never mind the trouble we might be making for ourselves if we go to face our Maker and our Judge unprepared.

We have already looked at some of the issues that were and are part of 'making a good end':

making our peace with God, making our peace with others while we can. But there are other more practical matters to which we also need to attend, and retirement is the time to begin, if we have not begun before. After all none of us know how short our time is.

First, there are various steps that we can take to make it easier for our next-of-kin to handle the legacy of our affairs when we die. The most obvious step is to make a will. It is surprising how many people put off making a will, perhaps fearing irrationally that making a will might hasten their end. But we ought to make a will as soon as we have dependents, husband, wife, children.

Many people have done so earlier in life, but wills go out of date. Retirement is a good moment to make a will or else to take out and revise the will that we have already made.

Although there is always a temptation to take short-cuts and use a cheap pro-forma, the law is full of traps for the unwary, and the money spent on having a properly qualified solicitor to draw up a will can save both time, trouble, and money later on.

The same goes for the appointment of executors. Unless our affairs are extremely simple and straightforward it is best to appoint a professional body, such as a firm of solicitors or an insurance company, to act as, at least, co-executors with a friend or relation, to carry out our last wishes. There can be a large amount of work involved in executing a will. Do we really want to saddle our next-of-kin with this work in the midst of their own busy lives? They will probably need professional advice, for which they will have to pay in any case.

My own father ended his career in the City of London as Manager of the Trustee Department for one of the big insurance companies. The responsibility of his department was to execute the wills and trusts of the company's clients. My father therefore had plenty of experience of dealing with the affairs of the deceased and the last lesson of many that he taught me by his example was about how to die.

In practical terms, he left not only an up-to-date will, but a sheet of instructions telling me what I needed to do and whom I needed to inform about his death, together with the necessary addresses and telephone numbers. All his personal papers were in one drawer in his desk together with a list of the utility companies that served the house. He had also sorted out his personal possessions.

The world seems to be divided between people who are chuckers and people who are hoarders. The chuckers throw away everything for which they have no immediate use. The hoarders save and keep everything, in case they might want it or need it sometime in the future.

The chuckers do find from time to time that they have thrown away something that they later want, but that is the price they pay for traveling light. The hoarders, on the other hand, have drawers, cupboards, attics, cellars, garages, sheds, and possibly even second homes, full to overflowing with memorabilia, papers, photographs, clothes, tools, broken prams and baby buggies, children's toys, their children's as well as their own, the accumulated junk of a lifetime.

I do not think that my father had ever been a hoarder, but when he died he left just a couple of drawers of his clothes and a couple of suits for us to take to the charity shop. Afterwards, when my mother came to live with us we had to sort out the household goods as well, but my father had done what he could to simplify our task. As much as he could he had lightened the ship and thrown the excess baggage over the side before he set out on his last journey.

It really is not considerate to leave piles of junk to others to sort out and dispose of when we die. It can take days or weeks or months to empty other people's drawers and cupboards, examine all their contents, decide about what to keep and what to put in the skip, ask the siblings and relatives if they want granny's tea-pot or grandfather's fishing rod, perhaps have the Crown Derby valued before sending it either to the charity shop or the sale room.

It is much kinder to do most of this work for ourselves before we become incapable of doing it, to ask our children personally what they want to have after we are gone, and to leave clear instructions about who is to have which pieces. More family quarrels arise over inheritances than at any other time. It is better to have family discussions, even conferences, about the disposal of our possessions, than to leave our kith and kin to fight over our goods afterwards.

It is sad enough when a parent or a loved one dies, without the grief being confounded with anger and envy over who got what. Part of making a good end is to prepare for it, not only in spiritual ways but also in these practical and material ways.

Amongst the instructions that we need to leave are those concerning the funeral. Discuss with your spouse or your children whether you and they want you to be buried or cremated. Some people have strong feelings one way or the other about this, and having weighed the options we need to leave a clear note of our wishes. We may have ideas also about hymns, songs, music, readings, prayers, or the lack of them, at our funeral service or committal.

As a vicar I always resisted secular songs and readings at a Christian funeral service. Other clergy are more flexible, but our requests must always be subject to the requirements of the church, the cemetery chapel or the person presiding at our obsequies. The family gathering afterwards is a better place to play the old Elvis

Presley songs that mum liked so much, than at the funeral itself.

A Christian funeral at least is not primarily a memorial service for the departed, but an act of worship offered to God, thanking him for the life of the departed, commending the person into his everlasting arms, and praying for the mourners to find comfort and peace. In this context secular and faithless songs and readings are a hindrance and a distraction.

Perhaps the most difficult decisions of all as we approach the end are those to do with medical treatment. Medical ethics and the law in Britain forbid euthanasia, the deliberate use of medical interventions to end a life. I do not believe that this prohibition should be relaxed in any way. There are too many temptations, on medical staff in an over-stretched health service or on relatives impatient to be rid of a troublesome old person or impatient to inherit their money, to open the door to the deliberate killing of the old and infirm.

Only the most ghoulish doctors or medical staff would want to be responsible for making such decisions or to be involved in carrying them out. As one doctor said to me, 'I came into medicine to cure people not to kill them.' No one's life would be safe in their hands, once the law or the profession's sense of morality condoned and approved of euthanasia.

But there is a greyer area in which medical intervention is withheld or discontinued, in order to let an illness take its natural course. Such decisions will probably involve not only those in the medical profession, but also relatives and the patient themselves. If I am a patient, I may have to decide whether to sign the papers to authorize a surgical procedure, or consent to a course of medication. If we are no longer competent to make such as decision for ourselves then it will be the responsibility of our next-of-kin. We ought to make our wishes known beforehand to those who will have to instruct the doctors on our behalf.

These are hard choices that the advances of medicine and surgery have made inescapable in the 21st century. We need to consider them carefully and discuss them with the other people who will be affected by them while we can.

The presumption must be that it is right to prolong life, because life is a gift of God and to be valued and enjoyed. On the other hand, we cannot escape death and we have to consider how to make a good end, and to some extent that may lie in our own hands.

Once we have reached a certain age or stage of life, we can make it known that if we die we do not wish to be resuscitated. A spouse or a carer ought to know if that is the case.

In more difficult circumstances we, or they, may have to decide whether to authorize interventions aimed at prolonging life or interventions merely aimed at palliative care. A hospital may be able offer a course of drugs that will prolong the life of a cancer patient by six months, but at the expense of debilitating side effects. Do we say yes or no to such a treatment?

It seems to me to be an open question that each person must answer for themselves. It may not be possible or desirable to make such a decision in advance, but one day each of us may have to make it. Whichever way we decide to go, it is important to know that God is merciful.

The advances of medicine have resulted in the raising of the expectation of life beyond anything our ancestors could have imagined. Someone who dies before the age of eighty today is thought to die young, and more and more people are living into their nineties and even hundreds. But is this all gain? More and more it seems that the years that we are adding to our lives are years spent contemplating our slippers in an old people's home, or enclosed within our own four walls and dependent on carers for our daily needs. Do we really want to prolong this period of our earthly lives any further?

It is not a question that we can answer for anyone else. Much depends on what we believe about life in this world and the next. If we really believe that we are going to a far better place, why do we cling on to life here at any cost? These are questions that may need to be asked and may need to be answered in very practical ways.

Winston Churchill, at the end of a long and eventful life, full of adventure, failure as well as success, honour and glory, complained in a letter to his beloved Clemmie that his last days were 'dull and grey.' It is a question of where our thoughts and hopes are fixed as we come to the evening of our lives. This world will inevitably become increasingly dim as we near the end of our earthly lives. There is no escaping that fact. But it need not lead us to gloom and despair, if we live in the increasing light of the coming day.

'The path of the righteous is like the first gleam of dawn, shining ever brighter till the full light of day' (Proverbs 4:18). And there is a mysterious verse in the prophecy of Zechariah, that Spurgeon, for one, took as a general rule of God's gracious dealings with us, 'When evening comes there will be light.' (Zechariah 14:7).

Some of our older Christian hymns, had a much more positive and hopeful view of death than is common today. Some of them are evening hymns that can be sung with the evening of the day in mind or with the evening of life. Here are two:

The duteous day now closeth,
Each flower and tree reposeth,
Shade creeps o'er wild and wood:
Let us as night is falling,
On God our Maker calling,
Give thanks to him, the Giver good.

The best is yet to be

Now all the heavn'ly splendour
Breaks forth in starlight tender
From myriad worlds unknown;
And man, the marvel seeing,
Forgets his selfish being,
For joy of beauty not his own.

His care he drowneth yonder,
Lost in the abyss of wonder;
To heav'n his soul doth steal:
This life he disesteemeth,
The day it is that dreameth,
That doth from Truth his vision seal.

Awhile his mortal blindness
May miss God's loving kindness,
And grope in faithless strife:
But when life's day is over
Shall death's fair night discover
The fields of everlasting life.

Paul Gerhardt, 1648

Making a good end

O thou most kind and gentle death,
Waiting to hush are latest breath,
O praise him, Alleluia.
Thou leadest home the child of God,
And Christ the Lord the way hath trod,
O praise him, O praise him,
Alleluia, Alleluia, Alleluia.

Francis of Assissi, 1225

Chapter Nine

THE EVIDENCE FOR
THE RESURRECTION

W. Montgomery Watt, said in his book, *Islam and Christianity Today*, 'By the standards of modern historiography, the crucifixion of Jesus is one of the most certain events in history.' We may be certain that Jesus died on the cross, simply because it is not the sort of thing that anyone would make up about their friend or the founder of their religion.

Crucifixion was a uniquely savage form of punishment that Roman citizens themselves were spared. 'Let the very name of the cross,' wrote the Roman orator Cicero, 'be banished from the body and life of Roman citizens, and from their very thoughts, eyes and ears.'

If you wanted to recommend someone to citizens of the Roman Empire, you did not invent a story about their crucifixion.

Crucifixion was a punishment reserved by the Romans for those generally regarded as the lowest of the low, habitual criminals, slaves and rebels. This carpenter from Nazareth was neither an habitual criminal nor a slave, so we can trust the witness of the Gospels that he was put to death as a rebel, for claiming to be 'a king'.

The fact that Pontius Pilate, the Roman governor, neither understood this claim in the case of Jesus nor believed him to be guilty of any serious fault is neither here nor there as regards our present enquiry. It is an historical certainty that Jesus died a shameful and agonizing death on a cross, as a pretender to some sort of throne.

It is also a fact that his followers and disciples, far from trying to cover up the manner of his death, eventually gloried in it, and made the cross a symbol of their faith, no doubt to the bewilderment of all their contemporaries, if not to ours.

There are some who want to deny the historicity of the crucifixion, but they are reduced to absurd lengths to maintain such denial. Muslims claim that it was someone else who died on the cross in the place of Jesus. But the facts are that it was the Jewish elders who instigated the death of Jesus[3]; these same elders witnessed his trial and condemnation before Pontius Pilate[4]; they then went out to verify his execution and to mock the imposter who claimed to be their king.[5]

Would these Jewish elders have been satisfied to see a stranger hanging where Jesus should have hung? Some of Jesus' own friends and followers also witnessed the crucifixion.[6] Would they have stayed to watch, and to bury the victim, if the victim had been a stranger and not their own Lord and Master? It was certainly Jesus who died on the cross.

Did Jesus really die, or did he just swoon in agony? The Gospels tell us that, as was usual in crucifixion, Jesus had been scourged before he was led out to die.[7] Some victims died from the physical shock of the scourging alone.

The execution was carried out by a detachment of Roman soldiers under a

---

[3] Mark 14:53-65
[4] Mark 15:1-15
[5] Mark 15:25-32
[6] Mark 15:40-41
[7] John 19:1

centurion.[8] These men were only too familiar, not only with the procedure of crucifixion, but with its effects on the victims, with the tell-tale signs of life and death, and with how to distinguish between the two.

When it came to the time under Jewish law for the bodies to be taken down from the cross in the evening, the soldiers found that two of the victims were still alive and that one, Jesus, was already dead.[9] Of the two who were still alive, they broke their legs. Such sufferers could then no longer push up on their nailed feet in order to breathe, and they died of asphyxiation within a few minutes. It was a standard way of hastening death in these circumstances.

The fact of the death of Jesus was then verified by a spear thrust to the side.[10] This does not seem to have been a random act of cruelty or mutilation; it was a means of confirming the death of the victim. The flow of 'blood and water', a separation of clot and serum, seen by the soldiers and attested by the other eye-

---

[8] Matthew 27:27, 31, 35-36, 54
[9] John 19:31-33
[10] John 19:34-35

159

witnesses was an indication that death had occurred.

One way or another, the Roman soldiers and their centurion were satisfied that Jesus was truly dead, and it was more than their lives, let alone their jobs, were worth to make a mistake. Jesus died on the cross.

His body was then handed over to his followers and supporters to be buried. Through the kindness of a friend, Jesus' body was taken immediately to a tomb nearby, hastily prepared for burial, wrapped in a linen shroud, and laid in a rock-hewn grave.[11] All this was only what was expected in a decent burial. A large stone, of a type that can still be seen in the Holy Land, was then rolled across the entrance of the tomb to seal it, and Jesus' friends and relatives went back to their homes or lodgings in the vicinity.

All this, apart from the extraordinary events of the arrest and trial of Jesus during the night before, was entirely in accordance with Roman and Jewish practice in the 1st century AD and there is no reason at all to doubt the story so far.

---

[11] Mark 15.42-47

That all happened on a Friday. But what happened next? As Jews, observant of the Law of Moses, the friends and followers of Jesus rested on the Saturday, the Sabbath. The Gospels then tell us that some women from amongst the followers of Jesus went to visit the tomb, as grieving mourners do, early on the Sunday morning, and found that the tomb was empty.[12]

Historically speaking, there is no doubt that the tomb was empty. As the following days and the weeks went by the disciples started to proclaim that Jesus had risen from the dead.[13] This has been the church's message ever since, and it was at the core of the earliest Christian preaching.

The Jewish authorities in Jerusalem, who had been instrumental in putting Jesus to death, were obviously embarrassed by this news.[14] If it were true, it vindicated all that the disciples had believed and were proclaiming about the Messiahship of Jesus, a Messiahship that they had rejected, and continued to reject.

---

[12] John 20.1-9
[13] Acts 2.22-24
[14] Acts 5.26-42

If it were not true the easiest way to disprove it would have been to produce the dead body of Jesus. This, they were never able to do. The body was not in the tomb.

Where then was it? The theory that Jesus had not died on the cross but merely fainted, had then recovered in the tomb, rolled back the stone, and strolled off, we have already dismissed on the grounds that the Roman soldiers at the crucifixion knew what they were doing. Had they even then been mistaken, the injuries, the shock and trauma that Jesus had sustained would, in the absence of intensive medical care, have killed him in the tomb.

The only other possibility is that some person or persons removed the body in the time between the burial on Friday evening and the discovery of the empty tomb on Sunday morning. This was indeed the first assumption of the women at the tomb.[15] But, as Mary Magdalene asked the 'gardener', who had done so and where could the body be?

---

[15] John 20:10-15

We may be sure that the Jewish authorities took every step to discover the body of Jesus, could it have been found. They were unable to do so. The theory of grave-robbers is as absurd as any other theory that we have examined. There was no point in robbing graves in 1st century Palestine. The only time in history when there was any financial gain to be made out of corpses was in the 19th century when medical schools bought dead bodies for anatomical dissection. That was not the case in the time of Jesus.

More than that, dead bodies were ceremonially unclean amongst the Jews, and the only day on which the body remained in the tomb was the Sabbath on which the carrying of burdens was prohibited. Such scruples might not have deterred people with criminal motives, but no such motives are perceivable, and no God-fearing Jew could conceivably have done such a thing.

The only remaining possibility is that the body was removed by the disciples themselves. This idea is completely incomprehensible. All the evidence in the Gospels, and indeed all the evidence of everyday life, indicates that no one was expecting Jesus to come back from the dead.

It had never happened before, and has never happened since. When we bury people in the ground we do not expect them to come back. Neither did the disciples.

There was indeed an expectation in the Jewish faith of a resurrection of the dead at the Last Day, that is, at the end of the world. But on that Sunday morning, as the women went to the tomb, the world had definitely not come to an end and they were therefore not looking for the resurrection of the dead.

It is difficult to see how, in the absence of any expectation of the resurrection of the dead, the idea of faking such a thing could even have entered the disciples' minds, far less inspired them to do such a sacrilegious thing as disturbing the body of the dead.

The Gospel records do indeed suggest that Jesus had prophesied his resurrection, but the same records also make it clear that the disciples had not understood what he was talking about.[16] Nothing that we know of the disciples' behaviour between the arrest of Jesus on Thursday night and

---

[16] Luke 18:31-34

the discovery of the empty tomb on Sunday morning indicates that they were anything but frightened, discouraged and despairing.[17]

Nothing that we know of the background of these men and women suggests that they were consummate schemers and actors. They were simple Galileans, bewildered and perplexed by a sudden and unexpected turn of events, unprepared for the shock of the crucifixion and not expecting any sequel to it.

But the empty tomb was not the only sequel. Later on that same Sunday Jesus started to appear to his friends and followers. Beginning with Mary Magdalene in the garden near the tomb[18], then to Peter in an incident curiously only indirectly recorded in the Gospels[19], then to two disciples on the road to Emmaus, then to all Eleven of the Apostles[20], then, according to Paul, to Jesus' brother James, then to more than five hundred people at one time[21], the last two

---

[17] John 20:19, Luke 24:13-24

[18] John 20:16-18

[19] Luke 24:33-34

[20] John 20:19-20

[21] 1 Corinthians 15:3-8

appearances not recorded in the Gospels at all. Paul adds, writing to the Corinthian church about thirty years after the resurrection, that many of those eye-witnesses were still alive and, by implication, available to be questioned and to testify about their own first-hand experience of the risen Lord.

There are such things as dreams and hallucinations, usually associated with states of consciousness altered by mental illness or drugs. There is no evidence that any of these eye-witnesses was mentally ill or on drugs, prescribed or unprescribed, and certainly not all of them at once.

Moreover, several at least of these eye-witnesses of the resurrection went on to pay for their testimony with their lives, including the apostle James the brother of John, James the brother of Jesus, and Peter. On many occasions, others were similarly in danger of their lives. Would these people have been willing to risk and to sacrifice their lives for what they knew to be a pointless hoax? What was there in it for them if Jesus had not indeed risen from the dead?

The evidence for the resurrection

In any case the testimony to the resurrection appearances of Jesus must be seen in association with the prior evidence of the empty tomb. All this eye-witness testimony was in the public domain within weeks of the events, and remained current for at least thirty years after them.

At any time, but especially at the beginning, this testimony was open to refutation by those who found the message embarrassing or inconvenient: they only needed to produce the body. This, as we have seen, they were consistently unable to do. The resurrection appearances explain the riddle of the empty tomb, not the other way round.

There is other evidence for the resurrection of Jesus in the witness of Christians through the ages. What is typical of stories of Christian conversion and commitment is a powerful sense of being met in a spiritual way by Jesus, not as a dead teacher, but as a living presence, demanding an existential response. Those who have said yes to this presence have experienced the grace of forgiveness and the beginning of a new life, a life that has often shown dramatic changes from the life that went before.

All these changed lives are additional historical and contemporary evidence of the reality of the claim that Jesus is not dead but alive, now and for evermore.

No-one claims that the resurrection of Jesus was an ordinary every day event. It was unique, and therefore it is not possible to compare it or criticize it with reference to any other event in history. But the consequence of that is that the one of whom this is said to have happened, Jesus of Nazareth, was himself a unique person, and not to be compared with anyone else in history, neither in the history of religions nor the history of the world. He was uniquely the Son of God.

It is therefore he who can speak to us with unique authority about life and death, and about life after death, and he does. Of many places in the Gospels to which I could refer, I want to finish this book, about the best that is yet to be, with some of the words of Jesus from the Gospel of John, words in which we all can find a sure foundation for a future hope:

The evidence for the resurrection

God so loved the world that he gave his one and only Son, that whoever believes in him shall not perish but have everlasting life.

John 3:16

All that the Father gives me will come to me, and whoever comes to me I will never drive away. For I have come down from heaven, not to do my own will but to do the will of him who sent me. And this is the will of him who sent me, that I shall lose none of all that he has given me, but raise them up at the last day. For my Father's will is that everyone who looks to the Son and believes in him shall have eternal life, and I will raise him up at the last day.

John 6:37-40

Amen

Lightning Source UK Ltd.
Milton Keynes UK
UKOW040840111112

201985UK00001B/2/P